The Coming Peace
in the Middle East

Zondervan Books by Tim LaHaye . . .

The Coming Peace in the Middle East
How to Manage Pressure Before Pressure Manages You
How to Win Over Depression
Practical Answers to Common Questions About Sex
Revelation—Illustrated and Made Plain
Ten Steps to Victory Over Depression
What Lovemaking Means to a Man
What Lovemaking Means to a Woman
The Act of Marriage (with Beverly LaHaye)
Anger Is a Choice (with Bob Phillips)

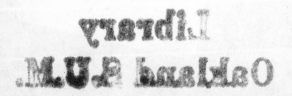

The Coming Peace in the Middle East

Tim LaHaye

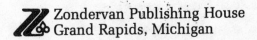

Zondervan Publishing House
Grand Rapids, Michigan

THE COMING PEACE IN THE MIDDLE EAST

This is a Zondervan Book published by the Zondervan Publishing House
1415 Lake Drive, S.E., Grand Rapids, Michigan 49506

Copyright © 1984 by The Zondervan Corporation Grand Rapids, Michigan

Library of Congress Cataloging in Publication Data

LaHaye, Tim F.
    The coming peace in the Middle East.
    1. Bible—Prophecies—Palestine. 2. Jewish-Arab
relations. 3. Near East—Politics and government—
1945– . 4. Bible—Prophecies—Soviet Union.
BS649.P3L34   1984   220.1'5   84-10454
ISBN 0-310-27031-6

Unless otherwise indicated, the Scripture text used is the New International
Version (North American Edition), copyright © 1978 by the International Bible
Society. Used by permission of Zondervan Bible Publishers.

Designed by Ann Cherryman

Printed in the United States of America

84 85 86 87 88 89 / 10 9 8 7 6 5 4 3 2 1

This book is dedicated to Carol Tubbs, a friend and artist of many years who laboriously listened to my concepts and drew them beautifully and intelligently so as to communicate the biblical truths I have tried to convey. Without her gifts of graphic design, the power of those writings would be reduced by half.

Contents

Acknowledgments

Traveling as I do—more than 180 days a year—writing is a team project. My secretary, Linda Matsushima, translates my scribbled notes in their highly illegible printing and types them at least three times. Michael Jameson and Frank York provide me the research I need, and trusty Jim DeSaegher checks my grammar to keep me from embarrassing myself. And Carol Holquist and James Ruark, my Zondervan editors, keep after me and give my finished copy their professional polish.

Many thanks to these fellow laborers in the Lord and trusted friends.

Introduction

The eyes of the world are fixed on the Middle East. Every day the headlines of all major countries carry lead stories about Lebanon, Syria, Iran, Israel, Egypt, Jordan, Saudi Arabia, other Middle Eastern nations, the PLO and Beirut.

Most of the world looks for war. Many anticipate a holocaust, for the hatred that burns in the heart of the Arab countries is a fire that could burst into flame at any time. Yet the Bible assures us that *peace* will reign in the Middle East someday—perhaps *before* the Lord returns.

One of these days the Arabs and Israel will sign a peace treaty that will bring tranquillity to that troubled land. The Jews will enjoy rest, safety, and prosperity unmatched since the days of Solomon. Unfortunately, it will be short-lived, for Russia will "think an evil thought," mount up its forces, stir up Arab hatreds, and attack Israel with the greatest army in the history of the world.

The threat of this attack will terrify Israel into turning to God for help. And their cries will not be in vain, for the Almighty will put on a demonstration of power unequaled since the plagues of Egypt and the parting of the Red Sea. The result? Israel will continue in peace, and the world will know there is a God in heaven.

It is an exciting scenario, one that could well occur during our lifetime. This book will help you to know what to look for in the Middle East—peace, not war. And it will enable you to understand why this writer believes it will happen in our lifetime.

1. Eyes on the Middle East

For more than fifteen hundred years the eyes of the Western world were fastened on Rome, Italy.

After the Reformation, westerners watched northern Europe, the spread of the British and Spanish empires, and finally the development of the Western Hemisphere.

Fifty years ago Adolf Hitler and Benito Mussolini were the focal point of world interest until the attack on Pearl Harbor on December 7, 1941, when the Japanese opened the world's eyes to the emerging oriental nations.

During the four decades since World War II ended, interest has centered on Russia and Asiatic countries such as Japan, China, Korea, Vietnam, Cambodia, and Thailand.

Today one area of the world more than any other draws daily attention from our press and television newscasts: the Middle East.

The Ancient Prophet's Predictions

The fact that after many centuries the ancient nations in and around Palestine have arisen from obscurity should not have taken any world watcher by surprise. The prophets of Israel and the New Testament two thousand to three thousand years ago announced that the Middle East—the land of Israel, Egypt, Babylon, Assyria, Persia, and the Hittites—would one day command the attention of the entire world.

If you were not alive during World War II, the Korean War, or even the Vietnam conflict, you may not understand how significant that prophecy really is. As a teacher of Bible prophecy for more than thirty years, I find the subject most rewarding to study. In the early days of my ministry I often pointed out that "Europe and Southeast Asia occupy our attention now, but one day the Middle East will take center stage of world interest." People would laugh or yawn with disinterest. One reporter asked, "Why would anyone be interested in the Middle East?" The answer is simple: Israel, Arabs, oil, Russia, and freedom.

The Prophet Ezekiel—2,600 Years Ago

"The word of the LORD came to me: 'Son of man, set your face against Gog [the ruler of Russia], of the land of Magog [Russia], the chief prince of Meshech [Moscow] and Tubal [a province of Russia]; prophesy against him and say: . . . 'Be prepared, you and all the hordes gathered about you [Persia, Ethiopia, Libya, Germany, Armenia, and other Middle Eastern nations, according to verse 5]. . . . In future years you will invade a land that has recovered from war, whose people were gathered from many nations to the mountains of Israel, which had long been desolate. They had been brought out from the nations, and now all of them live in safety' " (Ezekiel 38:1–2, 5, 7–8).

Until the late 1940s that prophecy didn't make much sense to anyone who lacked an abiding faith in the accuracy of the Word of God. Russia was a vacuous nation for centuries, and the Middle East was infested with warlike tribes and nations that made the entire area unstable.

However, certain men of God, even before the days of Peter the Great, wrote about the coming day when Russia would be a dominant world power and somehow unite the Arab states into a massive army of hate, advancing into Palestine to attack the nation of Israel—a nation that had ceased to exist in A.D. 135. How could these men speak so authoritatively about such a seemingly impossible alignment of nations? Because their study of and belief in the Word of God supplied them with inside information.

The Bible is a supernatural book, written not by men but by the Holy Spirit. The apostle Peter said, "Above all, you must understand that no prophecy of Scripture came about by the prophet's own interpretation. For prophecy never had its origin in the will of man, but men spoke from God as they were carried along by the Holy Spirit" (2 Peter 1:20–21).

This supernatural sign, often called "the predictive element of the Bible," has been incredibly accurate. During the days of Isaiah, Ezekiel, and Daniel, scores of events were prophesied long before they took place. So many signs were given about the first coming of Christ that some godly people in His generation were awaiting His coming—based on the prophets' teachings.

So it is today. Those who study the "predictive elements" of the Bible were not surprised when Israel was brought out of the trash heap of history and firmly established as a nation in Palestine. Ezekiel 36 and 37 have predicted for twenty-six hundred years that this is exactly what would happen. In fact, the regathering of Israel into the Promised Land occupies so much space in prophecy that were it never to have happened, or were the Jews to have become extinct during the eighteen hundred years they existed without a political homeland, the Bible could have been written off as a fraud.

Yet today I need not verify the simple fact that the eyes of the world are focused on the very land the prophets wrote about so long ago. Why? Because the Bible is a supernatural book.

Why Palestine?

You may predictably ask, Why should the land of Palestine be the world's focal point in these last days? Consider these primary reasons.

1. The Bible said so.

Prophecy is history written in advance. Someone has labeled it prewritten history recorded before it takes place. Only God can accurately forecast long-range events like that. But when once foretold, they must inevitably come to pass.

Some prophetic events were written, not on the basis of manipulations of God in the affairs of men, but on what He knew was going to happen. That is not the case with the prophecies of Israel and the Middle East scheduled for fulfillment in the endtime. They were written on the basis of what God would do to bring the world back under His direct control.

For almost six millennia God has chosen to permit man to live within the expression of his own free will. That is the reason for so much suffering, trial, war, greed, and expressions of man's inhumanity to man. If, during that time, an individual truly wished to find God in a personal way, he could. Jesus said, "If anyone chooses to do God's will, he will find out whether my teaching comes from God or whether I speak on my own" (John 7:17).

With the exception of the nation of Israel, which greedily subverted its opportunity to serve as a special nation unto Him, God has not chosen to manipulate the affairs of nations since the time of Christ. If a country's national policies were obedient to God, He blessed them. If a nation rebelled against God (as most did), it eventually brought damnation, suffering, and heartache on itself.

Not so the last days that are rapidly approaching. The closer we get to the end of this age, the more active a role God will play in world affairs. This was predicted not only by the prophets of the Old Testament and the apostles of the New Testament, but by Jesus Christ Himself. This world has not seen the last of the supernatural events arranged by God to prove infallibly to a skeptical age that He is alive and well in His universe.

The regathering of the children of Israel into the land of Palestine amid troubled times is one major step toward the last days. But God's supernatural destruction of Russia, which cannot be far off, is the giant step that will unleash an incredible chain of events bringing on the Antichrist, the tribulation, the second coming of Christ, and the millennial reign of Christ, when He will rule the earth during a time of peace that will last a thousand years.

2. Palestine is the center of the earth.

I believe another reason why Palestine was selected by God to be the focal point of world interest in the last days is its geographical location.

Speaking of Russia's plan to invade Israel, the prophet Ezekiel calls the Jews "the people gathered from the nations, . . . living at the center of the land" (Ezekiel 38:12).

In His creative wisdom God located Jerusalem at the center of the earth. This is confirmed in Ezekiel 5:5: 'This is what the

Sovereign LORD says: This is Jerusalem, which I have set in the center of the nations, with countries all around her."

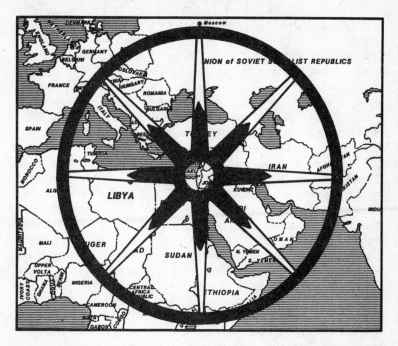

The original nations of the earth did not select their own land in which to dwell. The Bible teaches that each was located by God Himself. Deuteronomy 32:8–9 explains, "When the Most High gave the nations their inheritance, when he divided all mankind, he set up boundaries for the peoples according to the number of the sons of Israel. For the LORD's portion is his people, Jacob his allotted inheritance." God had a special purpose in locating Israel in the center of the earth.

This was confirmed by the apostle Paul when he announced on Mars Hill in Athens, "From one man he made every nation of men, that they should inhabit the whole earth; and he determined the times set for them *and the exact places where they should live.* God did this so that men would seek him and perhaps reach out for him and find him, though he is not far from each one of us. 'For in him we live and move and have our being.' As some of your own poets have said, 'We are his offspring' " (Acts 17: 26–28).

One principle about God we must always bear in mind when studying the Bible is that He loves *all* mankind and has consistently tried to win men and women to faith in and obedience to Himself. For that is the best way for man to live, both in this life and in the one to come. Consequently God located Israel in the center of the earth for a specific purpose. He brought the nation Israel into the world to be His distinctive "torchbearer," his special nation for evangelism. He intended that Israel obey Him so that He could bless her to such a degree that all the nations of the world would desire to know the secret of her prosperity. This only occurred for a short time under King Solomon.

The land of Israel was a natural land bridge between Asia Minor and Africa. People wanting to travel from north to south had to venture across this land bridge. As they journeyed, they would see the goodness of the living God demonstrated there. Thus Israel was placed on that land bridge at the center of the earth for evangelistic purposes.

Unfortunately, Israel sinned. Instead of evangelizing the nations around her and serving as the great spiritual blessing to the world, she disobeyed God and worshiped the heathen gods of her neighbors. Therefore God cursed Israel, and the land remained barren and desolate for many years.

Now, however, as God's prophetic timeclock winds down toward the last days, when Israel will be the torchbearer of the tribulation (see Revelation 7:4ff.), He is bringing them back into the land. Admittedly, they are still in a state of unbelief—just as Ezekiel 37 predicted they would be at their arrival. But their coming reflects the plan of God, causing the world increasingly to focus its eyes on the Middle East—the center of the earth.

3. Oil! Oil! And more oil!

Most people are sharply aware of the Middle East because the Arabs are sitting on two-thirds of the developed oil deposits of the world. All the developed countries of the world and many of the Third World nations are thirsty for oil. If the Arab nations' greed, nationalism, and fierce spirit of independence could ever be put aside, they could actually bring the world to its knees. But

COST OF OIL IMPORTS

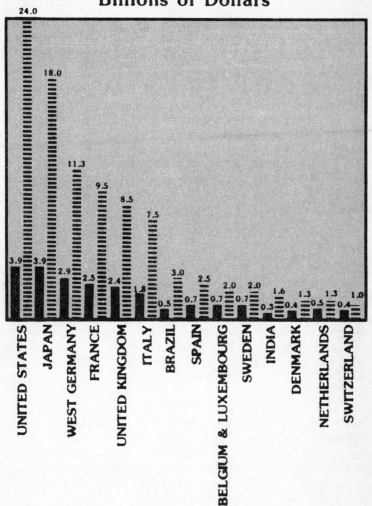

1972 BEFORE THE OIL EMBARGO

1974 AFTER THE OIL EMBARGO

Billions of Dollars

24.0

18.0

11.3

9.5

8.5

7.5

3.9 3.9 2.9 2.5 2.4 1.8 3.0 2.5 2.0 2.0 1.6 1.3 1.3 1.0
                    0.5 0.7 0.7 0.7 0.3 0.4 0.5 0.4

UNITED STATES
JAPAN
WEST GERMANY
FRANCE
UNITED KINGDOM
ITALY
BRAZIL
SPAIN
BELGIUM & LUXEMBOURG
SWEDEN
INDIA
DENMARK
NETHERLANDS
SWITZERLAND

their rivalry and political self-interest have caused them to forfeit probably their best opportunity since the days of Muhammad to have a major impact on the world.

No event since World War II has shaken the industrialized countries like the Arab oil crisis of 1973–74. What began as a hate campaign against Israel ended up in the biggest financial bonanza in world history.

Smarting as they were in late 1973 because Israel had—as in 1967—defeated the Arab armies on two fronts, the Arab countries placed an embargo on their exports of "black gold," and it was aimed primarily at the United States. They wanted Uncle Sam to put pressure on the Jews to return their newly occupied lands to Syria and Egypt. When they discovered that reduced oil output caused the price of oil to shoot up overnight, their greed for the enormous profits that "petrodollars" could provide took precedence over their hatred of Israel.

Most of the oil exploration has been done by the industrial giants of the United States, Great Britain, and the Netherlands. Fewer than one dozen companies have controlled the major development of the world's oil deposits. Since the early 1930s these billion-dollar oil companies have been making billionaires of Arab sheiks. The nomads' tents have been replaced by palaces, winter resorts, private jets, and Rolls Royces as the sheiks' lavish lifestyles have thrust them into the twentieth century.

At a price of $1 to $3 per barrel for crude oil, everyone seemed happy. The sheiks enjoyed an opulent existence that their desert economies could otherwise never provide. The western oil giants were among the most profitable companies in the world, and the consumer seemed happy enough to pay thirty-six cents a gallon for gasoline to indulge his long-time romance with the automobile.

The oil embargo of 1973–74 changed all that. For the first time, the Arab oil countries realized that oil could be translated into power. As they cut back on production, the price of oil on the soft market went as high as $17 by 1975 and doubled that within three years. Japan and some of the industrial countries of Europe paid as much as $45 a barrel before the free-enterprise principle of supply and demand caused the oil-producing nations to lower prices.

DEVELOPED WORLD OIL RESERVES IN 1973

137.1
Saudi Arabia

Two Thirds of the World's
Available Oil Supply
(390 Billion Barrels)
Controlled by Arabs
in 1973

MEASURED IN BILLIONS OF BARRELS

74.
Kuwait

62.2
Iran

33.
Iraq

18.2
Abu Dhabi

66.4
Other
Arabs &
Africa

Other
65.1

North America
47.2

Communist
Bloc
54.5

But for a time the Arabs felt that they had the industrial countries of the world by the throat. By nationalizing oil companies or demanding more control over them, they fancied that their possession of two-thirds of the world's supply of oil could buy them the advanced economies and standards of living of the Western world.

The shock waves of the oil crisis were as devastating to the industrialized countries, economically speaking, as any of the world wars of history. The more dependent on oil a nation was, the greater the embargo's impact on her economy. America, the world's industrialized leader for decades, was almost brought to her knees while the Arab sheiks continued to amass petrodollars, ranging from a $100 billion surplus in 1974 to an estimated $250 to $650 billion surplus by 1975. (No one knows for certain how great their profits were, not even their Swiss bankers.)

Admittedly, these Arab members of OPEC (Organization of Petroleum Exporting Countries) had to divide their *surplus income* among thirteen countries. To put this in perspective, we must recognize that the United States was the richest country in the world prior to 1973. She registered her largest annual surplus income in 1949, when her exports exceeded imports by $26 billion. The chart above indicates the vast extent of the Arabs' revenues. In their attempt to bring their undeveloped nations into the twentieth century in a rush, they lost billions in misguided ventures. Today whole buildings, apartments, and even cities are left abandoned in the desert, mute evidence that dollars can't buy made-to-order civilizations.

The sheiks of the Middle East realized before long that they should invest their revenues in other enterprises. All over the world, notably in the United States and Great Britain, Arab money has bought palatial mansions, hotels, business firms, and banks. Neither Western governments nor banking moguls know the full extent of the Arab wealth accumulated during the past decade.

While the Arabs were busy air-conditioning their desert buildings, the Americans were at home, heeding the counsel of President Nixon to lower their thermostats to 67 degrees and the driving speed to 55 mph. Nothing in the history of America has had so devastating an effect on the economy as the rise in OPEC oil prices. The country was so oil-dependent that gasoline rose as high as $1.79 a gallon.

Double-digit inflation hit all the industrialized countries. The more dependent a nation was on oil, the higher its inflation rate. The United States was the user of one-third of the world's daily output of oil; her expenditure for foreign oil jumped from $4 billion in 1973 to $24 billion the next year. For the first time, the United States experienced a serious problem in the balance of payments with no short-term solution. But no nation can continue such a practice for long without risking bankruptcy.

The light of optimism at the end of the national tunnel of progress flickered in the United States. President Ford began talking about "maintaining our ground"; there were suggestions that "smaller is better." President Jimmy Carter grimly expressed hopelessness for the future and predicted that Americans must get used to living with less.

The struggle to attain energy self-sufficiency for the United States began, amid conflicts among government, private industry, consumer advocates, and environmentalists. The oil companies launched worldwide explorations for oil on a scale unparalleled in the past. Congress authorized construction of the Alaskan pipeline, which was completed in record time and now can fulfill 15 percent of the nation's energy needs. Oil wells throughout the country that were not profitable to operate at $3 a barrel suddenly were working again. New oil fields were discovered in Ohio, Wyoming, and offshore Louisiana, Southern California, and Alaska. In 1981 geologists confirmed the finding of the largest known oil field in the world in the Beaufort Sea area of Alaska—larger even than the resources at Prudhoe Bay (the source for the Alaska pipeline) and in Saudi Arabia.

What energy crisis? Continually moaning about an "energy crisis" may serve the purposes of the Trilateral Commission, the Council on Foreign Relations, the Bilderbergers, and other international bankers, but it is really a giant fraud. Draining America's capital by forcing her to purchase foreign oil she does not need may serve left-wing internationalists whose chief designs are not in the best interest of the United States, but it does nothing to strengthen her economy. It does, however, pave the way for greater governmental interference with the economy, ecology, and personal liberty.

It has been verified in recent years that there is not and never was a shortage of oil. It is an imagined shortage to drive the price up and provide more governmental control over people's lives. *The Non-Energy Crisis,* a book by Lindsey Williams—a missionary in Alaska and the chaplain of the Alaskan Pipeline Project during its two-year construction—convincingly argues that Alaska alone has enough oil to supply the world for the next hundred years. Moreover, oil has also been discovered in the China Sea, Siberia, the Falkland Islands (a major reason for the war between Great Britain and Argentina in 1982), New England coastal waters, and other places. These relatively recent finds lead some experts to believe that many other oil fields are yet to be discovered on this planet.

Knowledgeable people who once grumbled about "energy depletion" and "the dire necessity of finding alternative sources of energy" speak of an inexhaustible supply of world oil—or at least enough to last through the twenty-first century, when crude oil should be obsolete as a source of energy.

Oil prices are coming down! The oil cartel called OPEC is rapidly breaking up because of the oil glut in the marketplace. When countries such as Venezuela and Mexico can undersell OPEC members, Middle East oil will gradually sink into a range that approximates real value.

Why are oil prices dropping? Consider . . .

- The principle of supply and demand creating pressure for conservation. Whenever prices skyrocket, people with limited pocketbooks are forced to cut back on driving, heating, and other use of energy. During the years 1978–83, even though the world's population was increasing, the use of oil dropped 20–30 percent. Now the oil producers are looking for markets for their oil.
- The opening of new oil fields, principally the North Sea oil reserves by England and Norway, and the discovery and development of the oil fields of Mexico.
- The success of the Alaskan pipeline. One expert noted that a special additive has been developed that speeds the flow of oil through the pipeline at twice the anticipated rate. Now the problem is to get enough tankers to transport the Alaskan oil fast enough. If that problem can be solved, the United States

could build another pipeline right next to that one, and she could become energy self-sufficient except for what she purchases from neighboring Mexico.

In the meantime, however, the United States and other industrialized nations are still dependent on Arab oil—which keeps the rest of the eyes of the world on the Middle East and gives that region political significance out of proportion to its size.

4. Israel is the third-strongest military force in the world.

World watchers are focusing on Israel today partly because of her awesome military capability. In a war between the Super Powers—the United States and Russia—Israel could provide the balance of power. Fortunately for America and the Western nations, Israel is completely committed to their side.

The source of Israel's military power is not the number of its troops. A country such as China has greater masses of troops, but the key to military strategy today is "first strike capability." How would China transport its hordes of troops beyond its borders? Her air forces are not great enough even to take on a small country like Taiwan. The diminished power of Great Britain was barely enough to defeat the undermanned and outgunned Argentines.

What makes Israel the third greatest military power? Her air force is inferior only to the United States' and Russia's. She is equipped with F-16 fighters made in the U.S. and with heat-seeking rockets. Her fighter pilots, trained in America, total more combat hours than their counterparts in either the Russian or American air forces.

Their flying skill was demonstrated in 1981 when the Israeli secret police—the Mossad—discovered that Iraq was building a nuclear reactor in Baghdad that was capable of atomic fission for military purposes. Israel dispatched her fighter planes for a surprise raid on the reactor plant. With conventional bombs they demonstrated their pinpoint bombing capability when the first pilot blew the concrete dome off the building and the second destroyed it with a direct hit inside the building.

In addition, Israel possesses the latest in U.S.-made tanks, helicopters, and other materiel and knows how to keep her forces in fighting trim. The Israelis live continually with their weapons "at the ready."

What is the significance? I have observed one fact about the Jews that may or may not be significant: The top three military powers in the world today include 90 percent of Jewry. As many as 55 percent (18 million) live in the United States; Russia and Israel each have about 3 million Jews. It is possible—and this is speculation on my part—that the Soviet Union may suddenly expel all her Jews before mounting the attack on Israel foretold in biblical prophecy.

Some will dismiss my claims for Israel as a military power because it is conventional might and not atomic. But if any country besides the Soviet Union and the United States has such capability, it is Israel, which boasts extensive scientific intelligence, education, and experience. Admittedly, the Jews have downplayed this possibility, even denying accusations raised a decade ago by the Arabs that Israel had developed an atomic bomb. The possibility keeps the world watching the Middle East.

5. Israel cannot be intimidated.

The Jews have their backs to the wall. They are easily the most hated country in the free world—hated, that is, by the Middle Eastern nations around them, just as the biblical prophets predicted. But after nineteen hundred years of wandering the earth, they finally have a homeland. They do not enjoy peace as yet, but as I will show in a later chapter, that could come very soon.

In the meantime, the Jews will not relinquish their land without a fight. They don't trust the Communists, the Arabs, or any other hostile member of the world's family of nations. Such fearless resolution has stood them in good stead from the time Israel became a nation in 1948.

Who Owns Palestine Anyway?

Palestine is the heart of the Arab world and the nation of Israel. Both Arabs and Jews share a common ancestry in the patriarch Abraham. But who owns the land of Palestine today? This is the question that ultimately divides the nations that form the Middle East.

The Jews maintain that the land is doubly theirs. They bought it piece by piece from individual Arab landowners as they gradually reentered the land during this century. In addition, it was given to them in perpetuity by God in the original land grant He delivered to Abraham (although they have long since forgotten that the condition for their living in the land was obedience so as to incur His blessing on them as a nation).

The Arabs insist that they own the land and have been cheated out of it by the returning Jews. Many fail to realize that the low prices paid by the Jews for rocky terrain and mosquito-infested swampland represented its worth accurately at the time. As the Jews settled in Palestine, they brought enough money to purchase the land, drain the swamps, till the soil, and apply modern methods of farming to the unproductive ground. Now it is a land flowing, as the Bible promised, with "milk and honey." But this does not mean the former owners were cheated.

Even Israel doesn't realize the full extent of the territory given to them by the Almighty. Yet they will possess the whole land during the Millennium.

"On that day the LORD made a covenant with Abram and said, 'To your descendants I give this land, from the river of Egypt to the great river, the Euphrates. . .' (Genesis 15:18).

" '. . .The northern border of Damascus next to Hamath will be part of its border from the east side to the west side. . . .The southern boundary of Gad will run south from Tamar to the waters of Meribah Kadesh, then along the Wadi of Egypt to the Great Sea. This is the land you are to allot as an inheritance to the tribes of Israel, and these will be their portions,' declares the Sovereign LORD" (Ezekiel 48:1, 28–29).

The Jews have never possessed their full inheritance, even under the praiseworthy leadership of Joshua and Caleb. They took the most fertile and pleasant land—the plains bordering the Mediterranean Sea and the River Jordan–that we know of as "Israel today." But they never occupied and exercised sovereignty over the vast region to the east as far as the River Euphrates. Had they done so, they might have lived in Babylon

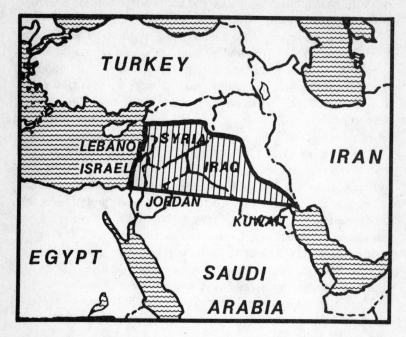

GOD'S ORIGINAL LAND GRANT TO ISRAEL

as her rulers rather than her captives.

An interesting sidelight in this issue was a comment made by Golda Meir when she was prime minister of Israel suggesting that the only mistake Moses made in staking out the Promised Land was in not locating it over the world's oil deposits. Little did she realize—he did!

Instead of possessing their original land grant, the Jews today occupy only a small portion of what God intended for them to enjoy. And instead of it being a land of peace, it has become a land of turmoil, suffering, and displaced people. The land of Palestine is not a "Holy Land," but a place of want and alienation. The "Palestine problem"—what to do with the displaced Palestinians—occupies the attention of the world today. Until a peaceful solution to this problem is found, the

Middle East will experience no repose. A solution will be found, as this book explains. But before we consider that, we will examine the other pieces in the Middle East jigsaw puzzle of nations.

2. The Characters in the Middle East Drama

To most people in the Western world the countries of the Middle East are a mystery. They shouldn't be. Many of them have lineage almost as far back as the origin of mankind and are located in the region of the first civilization. For centuries these lands were swept by wars, famine, desert sand, and nomads. Civilization largely passed them by and, until oil was discovered in many of these lands, they were marked by intense poverty.

Today most of the Middle East countries are still in poverty. Even those with the richest supplies of oil have not been able to improve the quality of life for the masses. Much of the wealth derived from oil has remained in the hands of the sheiks who control it.

One of the ironies of communism is that it foments revolution and incites poor governments to spend billions on military equipment at the expense of the poor. The standard of living in Middle East countries would be infinitely improved were it not for the everpresent threat of communism. The Middle East nations have spent more money for military purposes since World War II than was spent by all the countries of the world in World War I.

There are only two alternatives to this pattern: (1) Surrender to the Communist agitators, which would cost these people whatever freedom they now possess, or (2) the total removal of Russian Communism as a threat. And that is one subject this book is all about.

To understand these alternatives, it is necessary to understand the Middle East countries. A thumbnail sketch of each one follows.

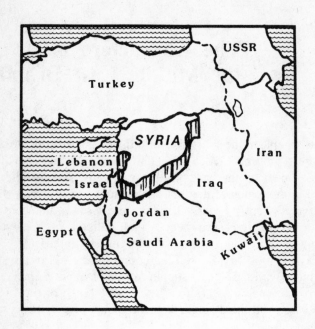

Syria

Head of State: President Hafez al-Assad
Capital: Damascus
Population: 9,100,000
Per Capita Income: $702
Land Area: 71,772 square miles (the size of North Dakota)
Religions: Sunni Muslims (70%), Alawi Muslims and Druze (16%),
            Christians (13%)

Bible students will recognize Syria as the area once generally inhabited by the Amorites, the Hittites, and the Aramaeans. At various times in history the Jews were at war with the Syrians; but sometimes they forged alliances, as when Asa, king of Judah, appealed to the Syrian king of Damascus for help in his fight against the king of Israel (1 Kings 15:16–21).

Today radical socialists rule Syria, spreading subversion throughout the Middle East. Ever since the socialistic Baath party leader Hafez al-Assad came to power in 1971, the nation has drifted closer and closer toward communism. She is virtually a satellite nation of the Soviet Union. The number of Russian military and civilian advisers has been estimated at upwards of 10,000. The Russians also have placed thousands of tanks, long-range artillery, MiGs, and SAM7 and SAM9 missile sites in Syria.

Syria's military buildup began in earnest in 1972–73, when she began to receive large shipments from Russia. To exercise her military strength in the region, Syria aided Egypt when the latter attacked Israel in October 1973.

Other Arab states have agreed to supply Syria with billions of dollars each year to bolster her shabby economy. According to the April 13, 1981, issue of *U.S. News & World Report,* Colonel Qaddafi of Libya gave the Syrian government $2.6 billion in September 1980.

Syrian troops entered Lebanon during the civil war in 1975–76 and never left. Until they encountered the Israeli army there in 1982, Syria had more than 30,000 troops stationed in the Bekaa Valley, supported by SAM5 missile batteries and hundreds of aircraft supplied to her by Russia.

When the Israelis moved into Lebanon in June 1982, the Syrians faced an aggressive foe. In four weeks of fighting the Israelis claimed to have shot down 85 MiG-23s and 20 MiG-20s, destroyed 19 missile batteries, demobilized at least 200 tanks, and killed more than a thousand soldiers. Israel had effectively defeated the Syrians and the Palestine Liberation Organization (PLO), but through pressure from the United States, members of the PLO—the object of Israel's action—were allowed to flee the country. In early 1983 the PLO and the Syrians began reinforcing troops in the Bekaa Valley.

Syria has been an enemy of Israel for a long time. She joined other Arab states in an attack on the newly created state of Israel in 1948, two years after she herself gained independence. Syria also participated in the Six-Day War of 1967, and Israel seized the Golan Heights area of Syria at that time.

Before World War I, the region of "Greater Syria" covered what now includes Jordan, Israel, Lebanon, Syria, and parts of

Turkey. It had been under the control of the Turkish Ottoman Empire for more than four hundred years. Before the Ottomans gained power in 1516, the area was ruled successively by the Seleucids (pre-Roman), the Romans (64 B.C. to about A.D. 650), and various Muslim potentates.

The Turks lost control when they sided with Germany in World War I. Once power had been wrested from them by Great Britain and France, "Greater Syria"was divided into four states under the League of Nations. France was given power over the Syrian state until it was granted full independence in 1946.

Turkey

Head of State: President Kenan Evren
Capital: Ankara
Population: 46,800,000
Per Capita Income: $1,140
Land Area: 300,948 square miles (twice the size of Montana)
Religions: Muslims (98%), Christians, and Jews

Under the Ottoman Empire the Turks ruled the lands that now include Syria, Lebanon, Iraq, Jordan, Israel, Saudi Arabia, Yemen, and islands in the Aegean Sea.

Turkey was one of the first nations to develop agriculture. Ancient peoples such as the Hittites, Phrygians, and Lydians had prosperous and powerful civilizations in this region.

Constantinople (Istanbul) became the capital of the Byzantine Empire after the fall of Rome. This empire dominated the area for about a thousand years until the Ottomans conquered Constantinople in A.D. 1453.

Today Turkey straddles the fence in her relationships with the United States and Russia. Though she is a member of the North Atlantic Treaty Organization, Turkey signed a nonaggression pact with the Soviet Union in 1978. She lies in a geographically precarious position, for to the northeast she shares a common border of 370 miles with the Soviet Union. Should Russia invade the Middle East oil fields, she would most likely come through this area. Moreover, Turkey has found itself an unwilling training ground for terrorists, who often use arms smuggled in from neighboring Bulgaria. Turkey has been a prime listening post for our military intelligence in recent decades because of her proximity to Russia.

Jordan

Head of State: King Hussein
Capital: Amman
Population: 3,500,000
Per Capita Income: $552
Land Area: 37,297 square miles (slightly larger than Indiana)
Religions: Sunni Muslims (93.6%), Christians (5%)

In Old Testament times, the Amorites, the Ammonites, the Moabites, and the Edomites lived in the part of the Middle East known as Transjordan. This land was vital to the ancient world as a trade route connecting Arabia, the Far East, Syria, and Europe.

Like most of the other Middle East nations, Jordan has a long history of wars. In the seventh century Jordan was conquered by the Arabs, then overrun by the Crusaders, and fell under Turkish

domination until she was taken over by the British after World War I.

This nation today finds herself in an awkward political position in regard to the United States. While desiring to remain pro-Western, King Hussein also wishes to support the Palestinians in the Middle East. It is difficult for him to satisfy both pro-Israel administrations in the United States and the PLO, but this appears to be his objective.

King Hussein is viewed by many observers as a mediator between the PLO and the Western world. At an Arab summit conference in 1974 Jordan and other Arab states voted to recognize the Palestine Liberation Organization as the "sole legitimate representative" of the Palestinian people. Hussein actively promoted the rejection of the Israeli-Egyptian peace treaty, and Jordan became the first Arab nation to break diplomatic relations with Egypt in March 1979.

It was also King Hussein who came under attack from Palestinian guerrillas in Amman in September 1970. He was ordered to leave the country within twelve hours, but he managed to rally the army and expel the PLO, which then established its base of operations in Lebanon.

Hussein must not only worry about external political problems, but subversion within. PLO radicals, who would like to overthrow his government, and Muslim fundamentalist extremists, who side with the Ayatollah Khomeini of Iran, pose perennial problems.

Yet the king seems to be trying to avert warfare. When the PLO terrorists were airlifted to safety from Lebanon in 1982, Hussein admitted only 267 of them. He does not want a "PLO state" operating within his nation, as one did until 1970.

Iran

Head of State: Ayatollah Ruhollah Khomeini
Capital: Teheran
Population: 39,500,000
Per Capita Income: $1,986

Land Area: 636,363 square miles (the size of Alaska and Arkansas
                combined)
Religions: Shi'ite Muslims (93%), Sunni Muslims (7%)

Iran is the once-great nation of Persia, whose history plays a
vital role in biblical events. In 549 B.C. Cyrus the Great united the
Medes and the Persians into the mighty Persian Empire. He
conquered Babylonia in 538 B.C. and restored Jerusalem to the
Jews.

Persia reached her height of glory under King Darius (500 B.C.)
when she ruled an area stretching from India to Greece.
Gradually Persia lost her influence and succumbed to the
invasion of Alexander the Great in 333 B.C.

In the seventh century Arab invaders brought the religion of
Muhammad. Still later the Mongols and Turks ruled Persia
successively until 1502, when the Iranian Safauid Dynasty gained
power. The British and the Russians showed an interest in Iran
during the nineteenth century. Russia desperately sought an
outlet to the Persian Gulf, but failed to gain control of the area.

After World War I the British were awarded a mandate over
Iran by the League of Nations. During the twenties Reza Khan
became the military leader of Iran. He abdicated in 1941, giving
the kingdom to his son, Mohammed Reza Pahlavi, the shah who
remained in power until he was driven from the throne in 1979 by
a coalition of Marxist and Muslim revolutionaries.

The radical Ayatollah Khomeini seized power in February
1979 and began to transform Iran into a repressive Islamic
republic. From the moment the Ayatollah took over the government, chaos has reigned in Iran. More than two thousand people
died by firing squads before the end of 1981 as he consolidated
his power.

Yet, as ruthless as Khomeini has been, Marxists and Muslims
even more radical than he have engaged in terrorist bombings
against the leaders of his government. Two groups, the Organization of Mujaheddin of the People of Iran and the Marxist-
Leninist Organization of Iranian People's Feday'een Guerrillas,
have managed to blow up nearly all of the original leaders who
brought Khomeini into power.

Subsequently Khomeini arrested most of the leadership of the
Tudeh Party Communists in an effort to protect his regime. He

also was plagued, however, with common banditry along the roads and threats from Afghani tribesmen along Iran's eastern border. Added to these internal threats is the Irani-Iraqi war for control of the Shatt al-Arab waterway that divides these two countries. In October 1980 Saddam Hussein of Iraq attempted to seize the waterway. A bloody war resulted in which more than 30,000 Iraqis have died; 50,000 are in Iranian prison camps.

Iraq

Head of State: President Saddam Hussein
Capital: Baghdad
Population: 13,800,000
Per Capita Income: $1,561
Land Area: 168,928 square miles (slightly larger than California)
Religions: Sunni and Shi'ite Muslims (95%), Christians (3%)

In Bible times this area of the Middle East, marked by the Tigris and Euphrates rivers, was known as Mesopotamia, which in

Greek means "between two rivers." The Assyrian Empire developed in Upper Mesopotamia; Sumer, Accad, and the kingdom of Babylon prospered in Lower Mesopotamia. Cities such as Ur and Babel flourished here. Some of the most ancient civilizations came into being in this area. Agricultural techniques, writing, city-state governments, sculpting—all these and more were developed and refined in Mesopotamia.

The history of the Jewish people is intertwined with the nations that existed in this area. Both Old and New Testaments relate the rise and fall of once-great empires in Mesopotamia. The area was conquered successively by the Persians, the Romans, the Arabs, and the Mongols. The Ottoman Turks gained control in 1534 and held the land until World War I, when the British took power. After the British helped the Mesopotamian leaders set up a government in 1921, they named their country Iraq and elected King Faisal I as their monarch. During World War II, she was ruled by pro-Nazi leaders, but British forces invaded Iraq and ousted them.

The Iraqis, as Muslims, are enemies of Israel. In 1948 Iraq joined with other Arab nations in attacking the newly formed country.

In 1958 a pro-Soviet government came to power in Iraq. A faction of the Baath Arab Socialist party has ruled this nation since 1968. The Iraqi government signed an aid pact with Russia in 1972, but relations between these nations has cooled somewhat in recent years. The execution of 21 Communists in 1978 was a factor in this.

President Hussein faces four major problems: (1) Soviet subversion; (2) Kurdish rebels fighting for independence; (3) continued friction between Iraq and Iran over territory; and (4) fanatical Muslim followers of Khomeini seeking to overthrow Iraq's "moderate" regime.

The Iraqi forces have not fared well in the war against Iran begun by Hussein in April 1980. Iraq is now seeking aid from the United States to rebuild her military strength.

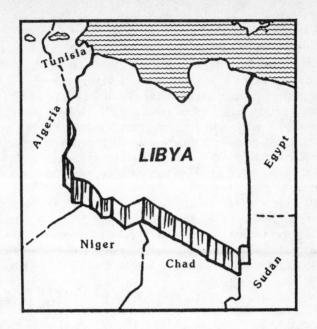

Libya

Head of State: Col. Muammar al-Qaddafi
Capital: Tripoli
Population: 3,100,000
Per Capita Income: $6,335
Land Area: 679,536 square miles (the size of Alaska and Minnesota combined)
Religions: Sunni Muslims

From the time Col. Muammar Qaddafi came to power in a military coup in 1969, Libya has been a breeding ground for terrorist activities throughout the world. When the Israelis pushed the PLO out of Lebanon in 1982, they discovered secret documents proving that Libya was providing the PLO with $40 million a year for subversive activities. Qaddafi even offered cash bonuses for every confirmed terrorist act committed by the PLO.

Qaddafi has also supported the Marxist Sandinista movement

in Nicaragua, Muslim guerrilla forces in the Philippines, and Japanese and European terrorist groups. There is evidence that he also dispatched a death squad in an aborted plot to assassinate President Reagan.

The land of Libya, first settled by Berber tribesmen, was ruled in turn by Carthage, Rome, the Vandals, and the Ottoman Empire. From 1912 it was governed by Britain and France, becoming an independent nation in 1952. Covered by the Sahara Desert, Libya remains an undeveloped nation. Not until oil was discovered in 1959 did the nation have any significance in world affairs. Today oil production accounts for 80 percent of Libya's income.

Pro-Soviet Qaddafi has apparently used the Soviet dictatorship as a model for his government. His nationalization of industries, currency restrictions, arrests, and general curtailment of human freedoms have driven the nation toward economic chaos. By mid-1981 the oil-rich nation had a debt of more than $12 billion.

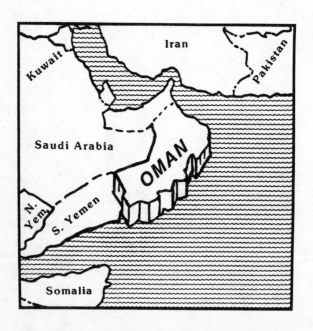

Oman

Head of State: Sultan Qabus ibn Said
Capital: Muscat
Population: 910,000
Per Capita Income: $2,400
Land Area: 120,000 square miles (the size of New Mexico)
Religions: Ibadi Muslims (75%), Sunni Muslims (25%)

One of the few genuinely pro-Western Arab leaders is Sultan Qabus ibn Said of Oman. Though Oman is small by comparison with many other Arab countries, she has a strategic location on the coast of the Arabian Sea. She also controls a portion of land that juts into the Strait of Hormuz at the neck of the Persian Gulf. Through this strait flows two-thirds of the world's oil production and four-fifths of Japan's oil needs.

Qabus is a strong supporter of American military presence in the Middle East and has encouraged the construction of military bases by the United States in his land.

Afghanistan

Head of State: President Babrak Karmal
Capital: Kabul
Population: 15,400,000
Per Capita Income: $168
Land Area: 251,773 square miles (slightly smaller than Texas)
Religions: Sunni Muslims (80%), Shi'ite Muslims (20%)

Foreign empires controlled Afghanistan throughout her history until the eighteenth century, when a native united kingdom was established. Britain and Russia competed for control of this region during the eighteenth and nineteenth centuries, but were unsuccessful. Afghanistan became an independent nation in 1919.

In 1978 pro-Soviet forces overthrew the government. After signing a twenty-year military and economic agreement with the Soviet Union, the "puppet regime" invited 100,000 Russian troops in an action tantamount to an invasion. These Russian invaders have been engaged in continual warfare with indigenous rebels. Unless the rebels can reverse the tide, Afghanistan will likely remain a Soviet satellite nation.

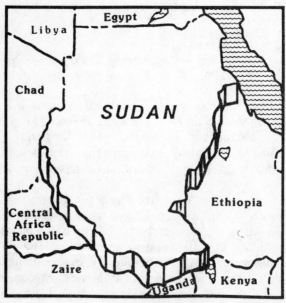

Sudan

Head of State: President Gaafar Mohammed Nimeiri
Capital: Khartoum
Population: 19,600,000
Per Capita Income: $320
Land Area: 966,757 square miles (more than one-fourth the size of
          the United States)
Religions: Muslims (66%), Animists (29%), Christians (5%)

Sudan illustrates the problems that have wracked many emerging
nations upon gaining independence from colonial powers. She
was torn by internal strife for seventeen years after the
Egyptians and the British granted independence in 1956. The
Arabs in the north and African tribal groups in the south warred
bitterly, leaving 500,000 people dead and 750,000 homeless.

After a series of military coups, Gaafar Mohammed Nimeiri
took power in 1969 and announced his intentions of establishing
a socialist state. Although he was originally pro-Soviet, a
communist-inspired coup attempt in 1971 caused him to draw
back from a close alliance with Russia. Today Nimeiri sees two
threats to his nation—the Soviet Union and Libya.

Niger

Head of State: President Seyni Kountche
Capital: Niamey
Population: 5,600,000
Per Capita Income: $250
Land Area: 459,000 square miles (three-fourths the size of Alaska)
Religions: Muslims (85%), Animists (14%)

As one of the countries lying chiefly in the Sahel, Niger remains
a poor and undeveloped nation struggling for economic survival.
Settled in the eleventh century by the Tuareg, Berber nomads
from North Africa, Niger eventually fell under the control of the
Songhai Empire in the sixteenth century.

European explorers who first came upon Niger in the nineteenth century found only widely dispersed, warring tribes. The
British and French brought Niger under French control in 1890,
and in 1922 she became a colony under the Federation of French
West Africa. She experienced relative peace during those years.

In 1960 Niger became an independent nation, but she has

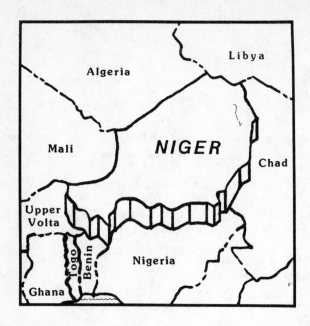

chosen to maintain close economic and military ties with France. Perennially plagued by drought, she experienced her most severe economic and human crisis in 1973–74, when famine killed half the country's livestock and as many as two million people from the Tuareg tribe. At the height of the famine in 1974, Army Chief of Staff Lt. Col. Seyni Kountche took power in a military coup and installed himself as head of state.

Chad

Head of State: Hissen Habre
Capital: N'Djamena
Population: 4,700,000
Per Capita Income: $73
Land Area: 495,000 square miles (seven-eighths the size of Alaska)
Religions: Muslims (45%), Animists (45%), Christians (10%)

Arab slave traders and other kingdoms ruled the desert nation of Chad at various times in its history. France took control of it in

the early twentieth century, and it remained a colony until it was granted independence in 1960. Since 1966 there has been sporadic warfare between Muslims in the north and animists and Christians in the south.

The current head of state, Hissen Habre, overthrew the government of President Goukouni Oueddei in June 1982.

Ethiopia

Head of State: Mengistu Haile Mariam
Capital: Addis Ababa
Population: 33,300,000
Per Capita Income: $117
Land Area: 472,400 square miles (four-fifths the size of Alaska)
Religions: Coptic Christians (40%), Muslims (40%), Animists (10%)

Ever since a pro-Soviet military junta overthrew Emperor Haile Selassie in 1974, Ethiopia has allied itself with Libya, Syria, South Yemen, and the Soviet Union. Ethiopia and South Yemen

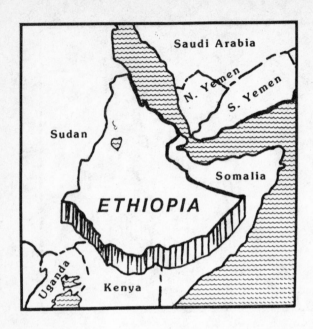

straddle the Red Sea and are able to control access of shipping through the sea and the Suez Canal.

Once a relatively peaceful kingdom, Ethiopia has been converted into a Communist state beset by internal problems. Eritrean rebels in the northeast have been fighting for their freedom, their land having been seized by the Selassie government in 1952. In addition, Somali tribesmen in the Ogaden region bordering Somali have likewise been struggling for independence.

Soviet-led forces, including 22,000 Cubans and thousands from Eastern European satellite nations, have been warring against the two rebel groups. There is evidence that the Soviets have used "yellow rain"—nerve gas—in the war.

Ethiopia is one of the few nations of Africa and the Middle East that numbers a large Christian population. A semitic people from Arabia moved into this area more than three thousand years ago. By A.D. 300 many of the inhabitants had been converted to Christianity. Although she was invaded many times by the

Muslims, Ethiopia remained quite free of foreign domination. Italy invaded the country in 1880, but was defeated; under Mussolini, however, Italy conquered Ethiopia and ruled her from 1936 to 1941, when the British drove the Italians out.

Emperor Selassie established a parliament, judiciary system, and the nation's first written constitution in 1931, but also barred all political parties. His power declined in the late sixties and early seventies; student riots, an army mutiny, severe drought conditions, and internal subversion eventually brought his reign to an end.

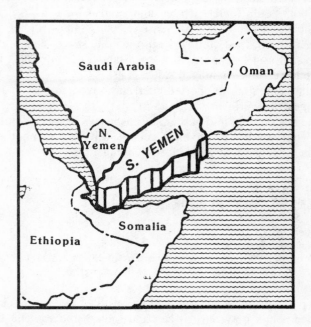

South Yemen

Head of State: President Ali Nasir Muhammad al-Hasani
Capital: Aden
Population: 2,000,000
Per Capita Income: $310
Land Area: 130,541 square miles (slightly larger than New Mexico)
Religions: Sunni Muslims (91%), Christians (4%), Hindus (3.5%)

The port city of Aden in South Yemen was once a vital British military base, guarding the entrance to the Red Sea and the Suez Canal. In biblical times Aden was also an important port of trade for incense, spice, and silk.

The British had ruled this area for more than a hundred years before guerrilla warfare eventually led to independence in 1967. Two years later, a radical wing of the National Liberation Front took power and began converting the nation into a Communist state.

The present dictator of the People's Democratic Republic of Yemen is Ali Nasir Muhammad al-Hasani. He has welcomed aid from both the Soviet Union and Red China in order to consolidate his power. At least 4,000 Cuban soldiers are stationed there; East Germans run the state secret police force. Ethiopian troops, Japanese terrorists, and PLO guerrillas have received extensive training in Aden.

South Yemen has supported guerrilla movements in Oman in the hopes of overthrowing Sultan Qabus' pro-Western regime, and she has entered into border skirmishes with North Yemen as well. The South Yemen air force of MiG-21s is piloted by Cubans, East Germans, and North Koreans.

North Yemen

Head of State: President Ali Abdullah Saleh
Capital: Sanaa
Population: 5,300,000
Per Capita Income: $475
Land Area: 77,200 square miles (the size of South Dakota)
Religions: Sunni Muslims (50%), Shi'ite Muslims (50%)

Once part of the ancient kingdom of Sheba, North Yemen provided a link between African and Indian traders. The Bible tells of the Queen of Sheba bringing gold, spices, and precious stones to King Solomon; but today North Yemen is one of the poorest and most backward countries in the world.

The head of state, Lt. Col. Ali Abdullah Saleh, negotiated with South Yemen in February 1983 to unite the two nations, converting them into a single Islamic state with a parliamentary democracy and a "mixed economy"—meaning part socialism, part free enterprise. Should reunification take place, the new

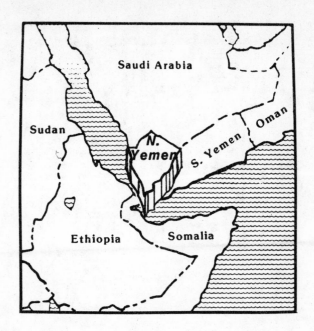

nation would probably not remain an Islamic state politically, but rather become a Soviet satellite.

Egypt

Head of State: President Hosni Mubarak
Capital: Cairo
Population: 43,200,000
Per Capita Income: $448
Land Area: 385,201 square miles (the size of Texas and Arizona combined)
Religions: Sunni Muslims (90%), Coptic Christians (7%)

The Egyptian civilization flourished for more than three thousand years before the birth of Christ, but the nation underwent gradual decline until she fell to the Persians in 341 B.C. For centuries she was dominated by foreign powers. The Mamluk Empire ruled from A.D. 1250 until the Ottoman Turks took over in 1517.

The British ruled Egypt as a protectorate under the League of Nations from 1914 to 1922, when she gained her independence. The monarchy of King Farouk was overthrown in 1952, and two years later Lt. Col. Gamal Abdul Nasser staged a coup and made himself president. Nasser was pro-Soviet, but when he died in 1970, his successor—Anwar Sadat—began to pursue a pro-Western policy. The climax came in July 1972, when Sadat ordered 20,000 Soviet troops out of the country.

In 1978 Sadat became the first head of a Muslim state to visit Israel, and in March 1979 he signed a formal peace treaty with Israel, ending thirty years of sporadic warfare between the two countries. He was assassinated by terrorists in October 1981.

Sadat's successor, Mohammed Hosni Mubarak, has continued to follow pro-Western policies. He has cracked down on Muslim extremists, many of whom have had the support of neighboring Libya. Many of the leftover Soviet weapons in Egypt have been given to Afghani rebels who are fighting against the Soviets in Afghanistan.

Saudi Arabia

Head of State: King Fahd
Capital: Riyadh
Population: 10,400,000
Per Capita Income: $11,500
Land Area: 927,000 square miles (one-fourth the size of the United
             States)
Religions: Muslims (99%)

Saudi Arabia is the birthplace of Muhammad, the founder of
Islam. By military conquest and religious zeal, the Islamic faith
and Arabic culture spread across the Middle East, North Africa,
and parts of Europe. The Arabic empire ruled until 1500, when
the Ottoman Turks conquered the region. In the eighteenth
century Ibn Saud, founder of the Saudi dynasty, overthrew the
Turkish rulers; his dynasty has ruled the nation since that time.

In 1930 the Standard Oil Company discovered oil in Saudi

Arabia and subsequently formed, with other oil producers, the Arabian American Oil Company to tap the vast resources of the Arabian desert.

The Saudis have been anti-Israeli and pro-American in their foreign policy, the Saudis joining in the invasions of Israel in 1948 and 1973. They supported the moves against Israel in the Six-Day War of 1967, but did not send troops.

In 1973 King Faisal was a primary instigator of the OPEC embargo on oil to the West. The embargo was an attempt to alter the pro-Israeli policies, but the effort failed in the United States. The Saudi government has supported the PLO in the past, but it has also been the recipient of much foreign aid from the United States, Britain, and France.

Saudi Arabia faces internal unrest from fanatical Shi'ite Muslims who support the Ayatollah Khomeini. There is also the possibility of subversion from Marxist and extreme Muslim elements among the thousands of foreign workers the nation has hired for the oil fields. Moreover, South Yemen has been a training ground for anti-Saudi groups.

Kuwait

Head of State: Emir Sheik Jabir al-Ahmad al-Sabah
Capital: Kuwait
Population: 1,500,000
Per Capita Income: $11,431
Land Area: 6,532 square miles (almost as large as New Jersey)
Religions: Sunni Muslims

From 1899 until 1961, Britain held control of this little nation bordering the Persian Gulf. Oil, discovered in 1946, is the mainstay of her economy. The government uses oil revenues to provide such services as free medical care, education, and social security benefits to her citizens.

Kuwait is under pressure externally from Iran, and internally from the large population of Shi'ite Muslims. The ruling Sunni Muslim leadership is not immune to a revolution such as that which occurred in Iran. With 400,000 Palestinians living in Kuwait, the nation is a strong supporter of the PLO.

Lebanon

Head of State: President Amin Gemayel
Capital: Beirut
Population: 3,000,000
Per Capita Income: $1,142
Land Area: 3,950 square miles (four-fifths the size of Connecticut)
Religions: Sunni and Shi'ite Muslims (62%), Christians (34%), Druze
(3%)

The smallest of all the nations in this survey is also the most turbulent at this time. Wracked by civil war since 1975, Lebanon was also the scene of terrorist bombing attacks in Beirut in 1983: at the United States embassy (63 dead), the U.S. Marine compound (241 dead), and a French military compound (58 dead).

The once-beautiful country experienced more than thirty years of relative peace until the civil war erupted. She had been a

nation of small principalities, each ruled by a particular religious or political sect. Under the National Covenant of 1943, power in the central government was divided among Christians and Muslims, with Christians in the majority. By the seventies, however, the Muslim population exceeded the Christian, with the result that the Muslims demanded more influence in the government.

The political and religious scenes in Lebanon are complicated. It has been estimated by some Arab experts that at least 96 and possibly as many as 164 different factions exist in the country. The most important are the Shi'ite Muslims supported by the Ayatollah Khomeini of Iran, the Sunni Muslims, Druze Muslims, and Maronite Christians.

When Jordanian King Hussein expelled the PLO from his country, the movement harbored in Lebanon. The Syrian army invaded Lebanon in 1976 as a "peacekeeping" force, and it has been there ever since, fighting against Maronite Christians and, after Israel's invasion in 1982, the Israeli army.

The Israeli invasion succeeded in trapping the PLO in its Beirut headquarters. The 11,000 Palestinians were able to leave the city and the country in a protected operation; but since then, PLO members have been gradually reinfiltrating the country.

In the meantime, Israeli forces discovered tons of Russian armaments stockpiled in Lebanese caves. One cave near Sidon was literally a Soviet military base with sufficient stores to supply an army of 100,000 soldiers. The Israelis also found maps and documents showing Russian plans to invade Israel on August 4, 1982.

Al Webb, a Mideast correspondent for *U.S. News & World Report,* observed recently, "Even without the PLO, Lebanon will remain what it was—a gun-happy society of feuding militias, political and religious parties, warlords, hoodlums and crooks. Prospects for the 'strong central government' that the United States and Israel dream of are dim indeed."

The Lebanese had placed their hopes for peace in Bashir Gemayel. Elected to the presidency in August 1982, he was assassinated only twenty days later, along with top government leaders, and Gemayel's brother became president. The future of the government stood in doubt after Syrian and Muslim forces took control of most of Beirut in early 1984 at the same time the United States was withdrawing its "peacekeeping" force of Marines.

The Middle East Puzzle

Although peace has not yet come to the Middle East and seems distant in the present situation, it will come. There is a common hatred of Israel that ties Arab nations together, but they also have longstanding political and religious animosities among themselves. In later chapters we will see how peace will be established between the Arab nations and the Jewish state. But a full understanding of the Middle East drama requires a close examination of Israel, the apple of God's eye. All human history began with Israel, and it will also end with Israel.

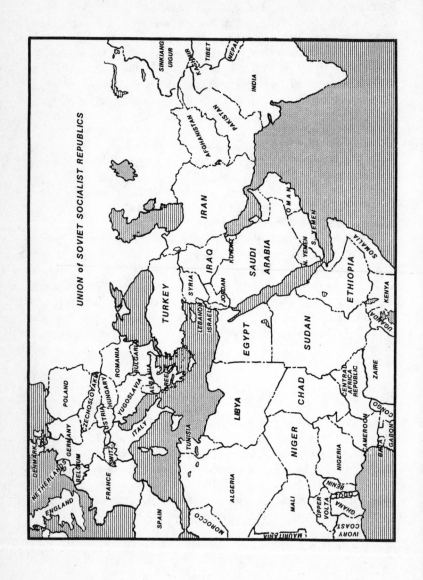

3. Israel, the Nation of Destiny

For hundreds of years, Christians and Jews anticipated a national miracle, the reestablishment of the nation of Israel in their ancestral homeland. The miracle occurred on May 14, 1948, when the United Nations officially recognized the State of Israel.

To understand the miraculous significance of this event it is necessary to see the history of Palestine during the past twenty centuries, from the time Rome ruled the land. The Romans, of course, were not the first foreigners to march into the Holy Land. As a natural bridge between Asia Minor to the north, Africa to the south, and Persia to the east, Palestine has long been a battleground for the invading armies of the world.

For Nebuchadnezzar to march on Egypt, he had to trample on the Jews in Palestine. He was followed by Cyrus the Mede and still later by Alexander the Great and other Greek generals. Eventually Rome succeeded in conquering everything west of the Euphrates River from Europe to Africa. Actually, in New Testament times—the first century A.D.—the land of Palestine was relatively peaceful. But subsequent history shows one conflict after another in the Holy Land.

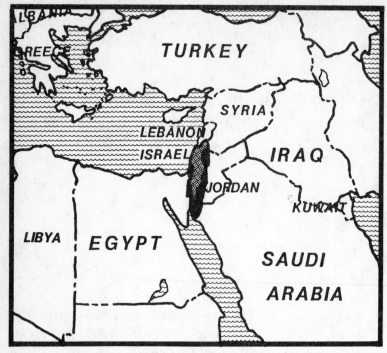

ISRAEL AND HER NEIGHBORS

Twenty Centuries of History

A.D. 70 — *The destruction of the temple*

Just as Jesus had prophesied in Matthew 24:1–6, Herod's temple
was laid in ruins. The Jews had tried to throw off Roman control
in A.D. 66. The Roman general Titus besieged Jerusalem for four
years and then left it in ruins in A.D. 71. Two years later Masada,
a Jewish fortress near the Dead Sea, was finally captured with
great loss of life. In all, the rebellion cost the Jews 1,356,460 lives
and 101,700 taken prisoner.

A.D. 135 — *The Bar Kochba rebellion*

The last Jewish rebellion took place when Emperor Hadrian
issued laws restricting the practice of the Jewish religion and

announced his intention to build a pagan temple on the site of the Jewish temple ruins. It took three years to quell this rebellion, led by Simon Bar Kochba. It is estimated that 580,000 men were killed in the fighting, and an equal number died of starvation and disease. Thousands were sold into slavery and dispersed throughout the Roman Empire.

A.D. *135–640 — The Roman period*

A new city, Aelia Capitolina, was built over the ruins of Jerusalem, and a Roman edict forbade the Jews to set foot there on pain of death. A pagan temple was constructed, and the province of Judah was changed to "Syria Palestina," from which is derived the name "Palestine."

A.D. *640–1090 — The Mohammedan period*

Arab control disastrously affected the face of Palestine. Under Roman rule the land was connected to the Western world, but Muslim conquerors cut off all contact with the West and established Arabic culture wherever they went. The stamp of Islam on Jerusalem became permanent with the building of the Dome of the Rock (the Mosque of Omar) and the El-Aqsa mosque; the city is second only to Mecca as a Muslim holy site. Consequently, the Middle East region did not develop technologically as rapidly as the West in medieval times.

A.D. *1009–1291 — The Latin period*

During this stormy period, Palestine was overrun on the one hand by Islamic Turks given to tribal warfare and on the other by the Crusaders, who in the name of a holy quest fought and died to regain Jerusalem from the heathen. Although Jerusalem was captured by the Crusaders in in 1099, it was later recaptured by the Arabs and became the objective of subsequent Crusades. Nothing lasting was really accomplished during this era. Historians question whether the motivation for conquering the Holy City was truly "holy" or political and part of European expansionism.

A.D. *1250–1517 — The period of the Mamluks*

Another unstable period followed the Latin period when descendants of Saladin the Turk ruled. Every Mamluk sultan was either killed, captured, or replaced by an enemy. During these 267 years there were 47 different rulers in Palestine, Egypt, and Syria.

A.D. *1517–1917 — The period of the Ottoman Turks*

The Ottoman Turks who terrified Europe were not successful to the north, but held control of the Eastern Mediterranean and much of North Africa. Their rule provided Palestine with protection from other foreign invasion for almost 300 years; but the land experienced many local wars.

In 1566 the rebuilding of Jerusalem's present walls was completed, and the influence of Islamic culture on the land further strengthened. The signficance of Jerusalem as a Muslim holy city is one of the thorniest problems confronting Israel today in her dealings with her Arab neighbors. Yet, as we shall see, the next Jewish temple will be built on the site where Muslim shrines stand today—the same place where Solomon's temple once stood.

The Elusive Peace

Jerusalem means "the City of Peace," but it has seen little peace over the last twenty centuries. Her land was instituted by God as a place of peace, prosperity, and blessing, yet she has been ravaged by war, suffering, death, and human tragedy. Why? There are two major reasons:

1. Israel as a people turned their back on the God of Abraham, Isaac, and Jacob and embraced pagan idols. Even the lessons taught by the Babylonian captivity did not turn the Jews permanently back to the faith of their fathers. Except for orthodox and conservative Jews, the sons of Jacob have often yielded to a secularistic, even atheistic, spirit. Brilliant minds have all too frequently been devoted to philosophies that have proved harmful to mankind. Consider, for example, Karl Marx, Leon Trotsky, Sigmund Freud, and John Dewey.

Nevertheless, a good case can be stated for the view that the Jews of history who have made the greatest humanitarian contributions to Western civilization have not been atheists, but God-fearing people.

2. The Jews rejected the Son of God, crying, "Crucify Him! Crucify Him! We have no king but Caesar!" In choosing Caesar over Jesus Christ, "the Prince of Peace," the people of Palestine brought the judgment of God upon themselves and their land.

One historian has noted that over the last nineteen hundred years, Palestine was so insignificant that it was not even a place name on political maps of the world. Her people were never conscious of a national identity, nor did they make any attempt to form an independent political entity. When the Jews were driven from the land by the Romans, Palestine lost its political identity and did not regain it until the founding of the State of Israel in 1948. Now the Arabs in Palestine are demanding something they have never had there in all their years of occupancy: independent statehood.

A Modern Miracle

Anyone who doubts that the modern state of Israel is a miracle must confront the question, How did the Jews survive nineteen hundred years without a national homeland and still be numerous enough to come to the land by the millions? They have survived genocide by kings and dictators, purges, massacres, dislocations, and deportations, yet they have maintained a national identity.

Consider the various forces which were at work to produce the miracle that, against all odds, has seen the Jews establish themselves in the land.

1920 British Mandate

A.D. *1917–1947 — The British period*

Palestine was under British mandate for thirty years after
General Allenby, representing His Majesty's government,
marched his troops into the Holy Land and received the Turkish
surrender—without firing a shot or destroying ʕa building in
Jerusalem. The territory included present-day Israel, the West
Bank, Jordan, and Gaza. In 1917 fewer than a half-million people
lived in Palestine, only 25,000 of whom were Jews. And fifty
years earlier there were almost no Jews at all there.

Encyclopedia Britannica explains that "Christian Millenari-
ans" of the nineteenth century stimulated the interest of Jews in
returning to the Holy Land, rather than any movement beginning
among the Jews themselves. Increasing attention among Western
Christians for the second coming of Christ revived an interest in
the return of the Jews as a sign of the end-times. Prophetic

literature began to appear, influencing the preaching, beliefs, and missionary vision of churches in the West. This in turn sparked interest among many displaced and homeless Jews. At about the same time, Baron Edmund de Rothschild launched a program of agricultural colonies in Palestine that proved to be both attractive and profitable to European Jews.

The Society for Colonizing Palestine formed in London in 1861. This organization and similar groups in France and Germany eventually helped to popularize the idea of emigration to Israel, but not immediately. Faithful Jewish believers met regularly in their synagogues to read God's promises to Israel in Deuteronomy and the Major Prophets. They prayed what Jews had been praying for centuries: "Next year in Jerusalem."

In the providence of God, a national disgrace in France was turned into an opportunity for the Jews. In 1894 Capt. Alfred Dreyfus—a French Jew and a loyal and capable army officer—was made the scapegoat for a serious military scandal. He was disgraced and sentenced to dreaded Devils Island as a criminal. It was several years before his innocence was firmly established.

This incident, drawing worldwide attention in the press, reminded world Jewry that even in a so-called enlightened nation that had championed "Liberty, Equality, Fraternity," Jews were not immune from anti-Semitism and persecution. They concluded that only their own sovereign state and a national homeland would make them safe from the kind of discrimination to which they had been subject for nineteen hundred years.

One wishes that all Jewish idealists would recognize that the secular humanist cause which they actively champion provides a philosophical haven for Communists and other anti-Semitics that will eventually undermine their purpose. It is hoped that one day world Jewry will realize that Bible-believing, premillennialist Christians are Israel's best friends.

The Zionist Movement and After

A brilliant Austrian journalist, Theodor Herzl, was deeply impressed by the Dreyfus Affair, which he covered for his newspaper in 1894. He convened the First Zionist Congress in Basel, Switzerland, in 1897. Jewish leaders from most of the

Western countries attended, and the following resolution was adopted: "Zionism strives to create for the Jewish people a home in Palestine secured by public law."

By 1914 more than 90,000 Jews were living in Palestine, and at least forty-three agricultural settlements had been established.

The Balfour Declaration

In 1917 Arthur Balfour, foreign secretary of Great Britain, issued the following declaration in an attempt to gain the support of influential Jews for the war against Germany:

> *Dear Lord Rothschild:*
>
> *I have much pleasure in conveying to you, on behalf of His Majesty's Government, the following declaration of sympathy with Jewish Zionist aspirations, which has been submitted to, and approved by, the Cabinet. His Majesty's Government views with favor the establishment in Palestine of a national home for the Jewish people, and will use their best endeavors to facilitate the achievement of this object, it being clearly understood that nothing shall be done which may prejudice the civil and religious rights of existing non-Jewish communities in Palestine, or the rights and political status enjoyed by Jews in any other country.*
>
> *I should be grateful if you would bring this declaration to the knowledge of the Zionist Federation.*
>
> *Yours sincerely,*
> *Arthur James Balfour*

Is it just a coincidence of language that the impetus to start the regathering of Israel was prophesied as "a noise and . . . a shaking" (Ezekiel 37:7) and the fulfillment took place during the world's loudest war amid TNT and gunpowder? I know from firsthand experience in World War II that TNT always involves great shaking. To prevent the possibility of stockpiles of P-51, P-47, and P-38 aircraft falling into Russian hands as the war neared an end, the U.S. government ordered demolition crews to destroy them. For two months the air base where I was stationed was "shaken" by detonating TNT as the fighter planes were destroyed. The biblical image indeed reminds us of dynamite.

As the ranks of Jewish immigrants grew and began turning worthless land into fertile fields, the Arabs there became increasingly fearful, hostile, and restive. Finally, in 1929 they made large-scale attacks on Jewish settlers. Riots and terrorism were common until 1936, when the Arabs rebelled against British rule.

The British had no patience for mediating the increasing hostilities between the Arabs and Jews who were under their supervision. Yet it became apparent later that the British offered a disciplined presence that kept the Arabs from driving the Jews into the sea when they were defenseless and few in number. By the time the British withdrew, the Jews were strong enough to defend themselves.

In 1939, under the pressure of constant unrest in Palestine, Great Britain reneged somewhat on the Balfour Declaration and issued a white paper favoring Arab independence and conrol of the area. Nevertheless, Jewish migration continued, accelerated by the persecution under the Nazi regime before and during World War II. By 1948 some 670,000 Jews inhabited the land.

Backdrop to the Current Crisis

A more detailed study of events taking place under British rule and after the establishment of the State of Israel is necessary to understand the current crisis and continuing conflict between Jews and Arabs in the Middle East.

Jan. 8	1926	Ibn Saud is proclaimed King of the Jejaz and Sultan of Nedj, which later becomes Saudi Arabia.
Oct. 3	1932	Iraq becomes an independent nation.
	1936–39	Emigration of Jews from Europe increases as Hitler builds network of labor and concentration camps, leading to the establishment of extermination camps in 1942. By the end of World War II in 1945, about 6 million Jews are dead in Nazi camps.
Nov. 2	1943	Lebanon gains her independence from France with total military withdrawal of the French by 1946.

Jan. 1	1944	France relinquishes her mandate powers over Syria, which becomes an independent country.
Mar. 22	1945	The Arab League unites Egypt, Syria, Lebanon, Iraq, Saudi Arabia, Yemen, and Transjordan, the first unity move among Arabs, having in common intense opposition to establishment of a Jewish state.
May 7	1945	With Germany's collapse, ending the European theater of World War II, the Allies liberate Jews and other prisoners from Auschwitz, Dachau, and other concentration camps. Worldwide shock and sympathy along with Jewish wealth from outside Europe spur the relocation of more than a million displaced Jews to Palestine. The process of assimilation begins; the area is estimated to have more doctors per capita than any other, and many have to seek other means of livelihood, including agriculture. Immigration further inflames the Arabs.
Mar. 22	1946	Transjordan attains full independence with the end of the British mandate.
Nov. 29	1947	The United Nations votes to partition Palestine into two states, Jewish and Arab. Jerusalem is declared an internationalized city, open to all as "the Holy City" of Catholics, Protestants, and Muslims. The Jews approve the plan, but the Arabs reject it.

Fearing a civil war, 300,000 Palestinian Arabs flee the country, abandoning their homes and becoming displaced persons. The United Nations sets up temporary tent camps, which become their permanent homes.

PALESTINE in 1946   1947 U.N. Partition Plan

(Left) Throughout Palestine, Jews and Arabs lived together. The British forbade further emigration of Jews to Palestine. (Right) Hostilities erupted between Jews and Arabs after the British withdrawal. The U.N. Partition Resolution of 1947 was intended to restore peace.

May 14   1948   The Israeli government officially establishes the State of Israel, with a population of more than 650,000 Jews, as Great Britain ends the British mandate in Palestine and removes its occupation troops. This turn of events is unacceptable to the Arab world; Egypt, Syria, Saudi Arabia, Lebanon, Transjordan, and Iraq declare war on Israel. The Arab armies outnumber the Israelis, but they are poorly equipped and disorganized; thousands of Jews die in combat, but Israel defeats the Arabs.

(Left) Israel's territory grew as a result of the war for independence. The U.N. tried to keep the peace by patrolling buffer zones between Israeli and Arab borders. (Right) Israel gained substantial territory in the Six-Day War, including possession of the old walled city of Jerusalem for the first time since A.D. 135.

Some 350,000 more Arabs flee Palestine, some to fight but most to enter the U.N.-sponsored relief camps. Many never return to Palestine out of fear of reprisals and refusal to recognize the State of Israel. Some Palestinians migrate to other Arab countries, such as Lebanon, Syria, Transjordan, Iraq, and Saudi Arabia; but they remain displaced persons, unwilling to assimilate and accept citizenship anywhere but in Palestine.

Jan. 7	1949	Israel has gained possession of at least 2,000 square miles of Palestinian territory, including the Negev Desert, bringing the new state to 7,000 square miles.
July 20	1949	The last in a series of peace treaties is signed, allowing a token United Nations force to help preserve civil order in Israel. The Arabs remain hostile and do not accept the U.N. agreements.
Apr. 24	1950	Transjordan—now Jordan—officially annexes the part of Palestine that has remained under her control after the armistice.
June 18	1953	Egypt becomes a republic, a military coup having removed King Farouk the previous year. In 1954 Col. Gamel Abdel Nasser removes the president, Gen. Mohammed Naguib, and installs himself in power. There follow years of harassment and intrigue against Israel.
	1956	Egypt, under Nasser, seeks to nationalize the Suez Canal after the withdrawal of British troops from the area. Israel invades the Sinai Peninsula; in eight days it reaches the canal and gains control of the northernmost point of the Gulf of Aqaba. Nasser suffers a military defeat at the hands of the Israel, Britain, and France, but gains a political victory by retaining control of the Suez Canal. Israel withdraws from the Sinai Peninsula.

Feb. 22	1958	Syria and Egypt establish the United Arab Republic under the leadership of Nasser.
May–June	1958	Civil war erupts in Lebanon. Peace is restored by the temporary presence of United States troops in Lebanon, sent by President Eisenhower, and of British troops in Syria.
	1962	The Yemeni monarchy is overthrown, beginning an eight-year civil war that results in the withdrawal of British troops and establishment of a republic in North Yemen and installation of a Communist government in South Yemen.
	1964	The Palestine Liberation Organization (PLO) is founded by Palestinian refugees to create an armed force for the purpose of compelling Israel to give up land for an independent Arab Palestine.
June 5–10	1967	The Six-Day War. The Israeli intelligence agency Mossad discovers Arab plans for a military attack and large-scale movement of Russian arms into Arab countries. Rather than waiting for an Arab assault in which she would be outnumbered 30-to-1, Israel launches predawn land and air strikes on Egypt, Jordan, and Syria. She destroys the Egyptian air force and navy and overcomes Syria in air combat; her tanks reach the Suez and capture Soviet-built missile bases intact.

With the military victory Israel controls the Sinai Peninsula, Jordanian territory west of the Jordan River (the West Bank), and the Golan Heights area formerly controlled by Syria; this quadruples her territory from 8,000 to 34,000 square miles. An additional 750,000 Arabs are displaced. The death toll in the war is 35,000 Arabs and less than 1,000 Israelis.

Of greatest prophetic significance is the placing of Jerusalem under solely Jewish control for the first time since the Roman era. Though this is not to be the last war fought over Palestine, the prophecy of Amos declares, "I will plant Israel in their own land, never again to be uprooted from the land that I have given them" (Amos 9:15).

1969   Yasir Arafat is elected chairman of the PLO, which helps to unite thousands of Palestinian groups and serves as a coordinating force for anti-Israel activity and terrorism.

1970   "Black September." The PLO attacks King Hussein's troops, but after ten days of fighting are expelled from Jordan. The PLO forces itself on Lebanon and establishes a base of operations for anti-Israeli activity there.

The arrival of the PLO brings Lebanon to front stage in the Middle East drama. Divided and weakened by struggles among Muslim sects (primarily Sunnis and Shi'ites), Druze, and Maronite Christians, Lebanon has provided refuge for thousands of Palestinians, but is unprepared for the PLO's establishing its terrorist headquarters within her boundaries. The PLO incurs the wrath of the Israelis with attacks on civilian targets such as buses and school buildings. The Jews retaliate with a show of force, but since they rarely succeed in

finding the PLO perpetrators, their vic-
tims often prove to be Lebanese villag-
ers; whenever they destroy a PLO command post, it usually turns out to be a
Lebanese home or apartment.

Oct. 6   1973   The Yom Kippur War begins. The only
time the Israeli military leadership
shows a lack of readiness is during an
attack by Syria and Egypt while the
Jews are in their synagogues observing
the Day of Atonement, Yom Kippur.
Once again the Arabs, equipped with
Russian armament, attack Israel in
simultaneous operations, Egypt seizing
large portions of the Sinai and Syria
taking the Golan Heights. But Israel
breaks through enemy lines, crosses the
Suez Canal, and cuts off the advancing
Egyptian army; at the same time she
retakes the Golan Heights, drives into
Syria, and would conquer Damascus but
for the U.N. cease-fire.

Although Israel wins this war, as she
did previous ones, she suffers her greatest casualties; what took only six days in
1967 takes nearly three weeks this time,
ending with a cease-fire imposed by the
United Nations on October 24. Israel
retains the Golan Heights and the Gaza
Strip and vows never again to be taken
by surprise.

1973

1975   Civil war breaks out in Lebanon amid sectarian rivalries exacerbated by the presence of the PLO. Yasir Arafat's strategy for the PLO is to base the terrorists in civilian population centers as a deterrent against retaliatory attacks by Israel.

1976   Syria, which has always considered her a part of "Greater Syria," invades Lebanon with a large "peacekeeping" force. The Syrians soon control 60 percent of the country, and for all practical purposes the PLO controls the rest.

Nov. 19   1977   In an unprecedented show of
                        statesmanship, Anwar Sadat, president
                        of Egypt since 1970, flies to Israel to
                        explore the possibility of making peace.
                        The historic flight is the first official
                        recognition of Israel by an Arab head of
                        state. Sadat, who had earlier reversed
                        Nasser's pro-Soviet policy, becomes an
                        outcast among his fellow Arabs but a
                        hero to the West.

Sept. 17   1978   At a conference hosted by U.S.
                        President Jimmy Carter at Camp David,
                        Maryland, President Sadat of Egypt and
                        Prime Minister Menachem Begin of
                        Israel sign agreements known as the
                        Camp David accords. This leads to a
                        peace treaty signed by Sadat and Begin
                        on March 26, 1979.

Jan. 17   1979   Just a few years after celebrating the
                        2,500th anniversary of the Persian
                        Empire, the shah, Mohammed Reza
                        Pahlevi, is forced into exile by Muslim
                        extremists. The shah goes first to Egypt,
                        then to Central America, and finally to
                        the United States, for special surgery. A
                        new Islamic republic is established by
                        the Ayatollah Ruhollah Khomeini, a
                        Muslim extremist who had become
                        endeared to Communists in both France
                        and Russia during fifteen years of exile.

May 27   1979   In keeping with the Camp David
                        accords, Israel officially withdraws its
                        troops from the city of El Arish and the
                        northwestern portion of the Sinai and
                        returns them to Egypt. The event is
                        marked by moderate violence as Israeli
                        soldiers struggle to evict Jewish settlers.

Nov. 4	1979	After staging large-scale student rioting, the Iranian government permits a mob to seize the embassy of the United States in Teheran, taking more than fifty Americans hostage for a total of 444 days.
Apr. 25	1980	Eight Americans die in a helicopter-airplane crash in Iran during an abortive attempt to rescue the Americans held hostage in the U.S. embassy.
Sept. 22	1980	Iraqi fighter-bombers attack ten Iranian airfields in a dispute over ownership of the Shatt al-Arab Waterway to the Persian Gulf. The incident, following numerous border clashes, touches off full-scale war between the two countries.
Jan. 7	1981	In a daring early morning raid on Baghdad, siux hundred miles north of their air base, seven Israeli F-16 fighters, with seven F-15s flying cover (speaking Arabic on their radios so that they would be mistaken for Jordanians), destroy the French-built nuclear generator in Iraq. With but a single life lost (a Fench technician), the Israeli air force sets the plant's completion back at least three years—if France decides to pursue construction again.

Israel's reason is that if they do not stop the Iraqis now, Iraq will use the plutonium generator to build atomic weapons with which to destroy Israel. Thus the military action is labeled "self-defense." Formally the world (including the United Staes) is outraged, but secretly many leaders admire Israel's courage and awesome demonstration of

bombing accuracy, and they are relieved
that hostile and unpredictable Iraq will
not join the nations with nuclear capability for a while at least.

Jan. 20   1981   Iran finally releases the Americans held
hostage at the U.S. embassy in Teheran,
some thirty minutes after Ronald
Reagan is sworn in as the new president
of the United States.

Aug. 7   1981   Saudi Arabia offers an eight-point peace
plan that essentially calls for a state for
Palestinian Arabs and a pullback by
Israel to the 1967 boundaries, including
complete withdrawal from the Sinai, but
excluding recognition for the State of
Israel.

Oct. 6   1981   President Sadat of Egypt is assassinated
while reviewing a military parade, an
incident attributed to Arabs opposed to
Sadat's friendly attitude toward Israel.
Hosni Mubarak, Sadat's successor,
tempers the friendship with Israel by
opening Egypt's borders to Libya and
inviting Russian technicians to return.
Yet he also reaffirms the Camp David
accords.

Dec. 3   1981   The FBI and Secret Service uncover and
thwart Libyan plans to assassinate
President Reagan by means of a five-
man "hit squad" that has infiltrated the
United States.

Dec. 11–28 1981   Three officials in the Khomeini
government are assassinated by
Mujahedeen terrorists in Iran, raising to
more than a thousand the death toll of
religious and government officials
murdered since the removal of President

Abolhassan Bani-Sadr from office in June 1981.

Dec. 14   1981   The Israelis seize control of the Golan Heights for defensive purposes. The U.N. Security Council, including the United States, promptly condemns the action and threatens sanctions.

June 6   1982   Israeli troops invade southern Lebanon in an effort to destroy PLO strongholds there. On June 9 they shoot down twenty-two Syrian jets and destroy Syrian missile batteries erected in the Bekaa Valley. Fighting erupts again following a cease-fire on June 12, and the PLO is surrounded in West Beirut by Israeli and Lebanese forces. At the urging of the United States, Israel allows the PLO to withdraw on the condition that a twenty-five-mile-wide buffer zone be established with an international peacekeeping force.

June 27   1982   Israel issues a three-point peace plan that calls for an Israeli-enforced cease-fire, Lebanese army control of West Beirut, and the expulsion of the PLO from the country. Syrian troops, which were already in Lebanon, engage Israeli troops but lose aircraft in a ratio of 79 to 1. Many Lebanese citizens welcome the occupation by the Israelis and the removal of the PLO.

Aug. 23   1982   After ten weeks of fierce fighting around Beirut, the PLO agrees to withdraw from the city. Several Arab countries reluctantly receive refugees, hoping the PLO will be assimilated with their people. Although the twelve-year presence of the PLO in Lebanon has

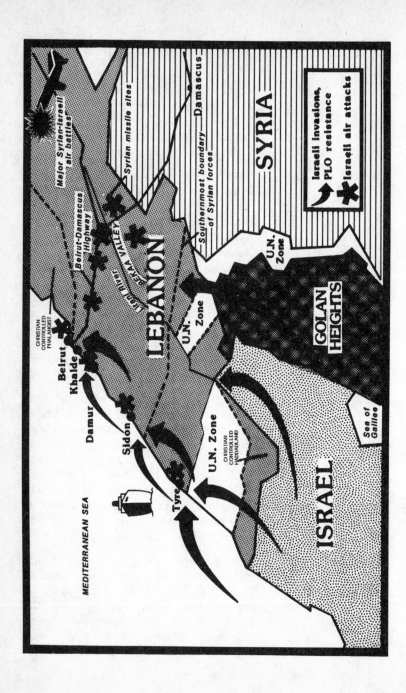

ended, fighting continues in the civil war, aggravated by the presence of Syrian and Israeli troops.

Aug. 27   1982   An international peacekeeping force arrives in Lebanon, including 800 United States Marines and troops from France and other countries. The objective is to encourage all combatant foreign troops to leave and to institute free elections with the restoration of civil order.

Sept. 14   1982   Bashir Gemayel is assassinated just twenty days after becoming president of Lebanon and seeking to bring political stability in a country still occupied by 60,000 Syrian troops and 45,000 Israelis. Gemayel is succeeded by his brother, Amin.

Sept. 16–17 1982   In civil unrest resulting from Gemayel's assassination, Phalangist militiamen massacre an estimated 1,000 to 3,000 Palestinians interned in two camps south of Beirut. Gen. Ariel Sharon, Israeli defense minister, ultimately is forced to resign his position as a result of the incident, since Israeli troops were to guarantee the peace and safeguard the civilian population.

Apr. 18   1983   A terrorist bomb blows up the United States embassy in Beirut, killing 61 people, including 17 Americans.

Oct. 23   1983   A truck bomb blows up the U.S. Marine compound at the Beirut airport, killing almost 240 Marines. A similar "suicide mission" at the French compound leaves 56 French soldiers dead. The bombings shatter a fragile and tentative cease-fire that began September 26 and spark new fighting among Lebanon's rival factions.

Israel's Future?

The powderkeg of Middle East politics continues. Peace has not yet come to Lebanon, the Palestine Liberation Organization still wanders homeless, and although the "safety zone" around Israel's borders is a little wider now, the peace that is predicted for Israel in Ezekiel 38 is still a distant dream. The tragic land of Palestine is destined for more tension, bitterness, and conflict until some kind of peace treaty between Israel and all the Arab nations is achieved. And that is the subject of the next two chapters.

4. The Future of Israel

"Now learn this lesson from the fig tree: As soon as its twigs get tender and its leaves come out, you know that summer is near. Even so, when you see all these things, you know that it is near, right at the door" (Matthew 24:32–33).

Many careful students of prophecy believe that Israel is the "fig tree" mentioned by Jesus. The nation of Israel was often referred to symbolically as a fig tree by the Hebrew prophets, and Jesus was fully aware of their writings. The disciples asked the question "What will be the sign of your coming and of the end of the age?" In Jesus' response, the fig tree was a clue that Israel provided something significant to look for. Jesus may have meant that the regathering of Israel into the land was *the sign* that His coming would take place soon and that "the end of the age" was at hand.

How Soon?

Whenever we speak of "the end of the age" or "the coming of Christ," the question most frequently asked is, "When?" Jesus' answer was, "This generation [that sees the fig tree] will certainly not pass away until all these things have happened" (Matthew 24:34). Very simply, the generation that was old enough to see and understand Israel's regathering into the land under statehood in 1948 will not pass away until the Lord returns and the age has come to an end. This is exciting!

How long is a generation? Most Bible scholars suggest it represents a period of thirty-three to forty years. Yet Christ did not say that He would come in the usual period of a generation, but rather that the generation which saw these events would not pass away. This suggests a longer period. Moses tells us that the average span of a person's life is seventy to eighty years.

> The length of our days is seventy years—
> or eighty, if we have the strength;
> yet their span is but trouble and sorrow,
> for they quickly pass, and we fly away (Psalm 90:10).

A reasonable conclusion, therefore, is that people who were ten to eighteen years of age in 1948, when Israel became a sovereign state, will not pass away until the Lord has come and this age is completed. We must be very careful not to set a specific "day or hour," for Jesus said, "No one knows about that day or hour" (Matthew 24:36). But we can know "the season" or lifetime, and many believe it exists right now. If this is the correct interpretation of Matthew 24, Christ may come in our lifetime. Certainly we should live every day with that possibility in mind, for nothing could hinder Him from coming today—or tomorrow— or next year.

On the other hand, nothing could keep Him from waiting until 1990 or the year 2000. We do not know the day or the hour or even the year. But if any generation had logical reason based on biblical prophecy to assume that the Lord Jesus Christ would come in its lifetime, it is ours.

World War I—Another Possibility

Many Bible teachers of the past generation believed that World War I (1914–18) was the fulfillment of "the sign" of the end of the age. Dr. David L. Cooper, president of the Biblical Research Society, was an advocate of that view, which is expounded in my book *The Beginning of the End*. The view offers the scenario that World War I contains the four marks of the end of the age declared by Christ in Matthew 24:7.

1. *Scripture:* "Nation shall rise against nation, and kingdom against kingdom . . ."

   Interpretation: A world war started by two nations engulfing the whole world.

2. *Scripture:* "There shall be famines . . ."
   Interpretation: The world's greatest famines occurred as a result of World War I.
3. *Scripture:* ". . . and pestilences . . .
   Interpretation: Widespread plagues during and after World War I.
4. *Scripture:* ". . . and earthquakes, in divers places" [1]
   Interpretation: Multiple earthquakes were first recorded after World War I.

If this fascinating interpretation is the correct one, our time on the earth is even more limited. The life expectancy for those who "saw" the first world war is rapidly running out. We meet fewer and fewer people who grew up during World War I (old enough to be aware of the events, but too young to participate in them). But though they are passing away, they won't *all* be gone before our Lord comes again *if* that is the correct interpretation.

Which interpretation—World War I or the founding of the State of Israel—is the correct one relating to Matthew 24:7 will be soon be made clear. In either case, we should be aware that our time to serve Christ in this present world is limited.

The Nation of Israel—A Miracle

We have observed two reasons why Israel's statehood is nothing less than a miracle: (1) If there are enough Jews to form a nation after nearly 1,900 years of homelessness, that is miraculous; (2) If a little nation of zero in 1870, some 650,000 in 1948, and 3,000,000 in 1984 can become the third-strongest military power in the world—often while waging battles against overwhelming numerical odds—that is also a miracle.

On June 5, 1967, an American engineer, sick in bed with the flu, learned from the television news that Israel had been attacked by her Arab neighbors to the north and by Egyptians to

---

[1] King James Version.

the south. With the zeal of a confirmed skeptic he decided to "watch the Arabs, who outnumbered the Israelis fifty to one, drive the Jews into the sea."

Months earlier, this engineer had been invited to our church in San Diego by a colleague. The night he attended I preached the sermon "Israel—the Infallible Sign of Christ's Soon Return." He was fascinated by the idea that the nation of Israel was not an accident of history, that God had supernaturally spared the Jews from extinction through almost 1,900 years without a homeland. Prior to this, no ethnic national group had been able to retain its national identity more than 500 years after being uprooted from its base, particularly if it was not relocated en masse to another place. The Jews were not only uprooted, but scattered into all the major countries of the world—yet they were not absorbed and assimilated so as to lose their identity.

When I began to teach the prophecies of the Old Testament that show how God would gather the nation into the land once again, the engineer scoffed. As the newscast described Syria's moving against Israel with modern Russian tanks and materiel, he was certain the prophecies would be proved wrong. Then, before his eyes, the miracle of the "Six-Day War" unfolded. What he expected would be a cruel death for a nation only nineteen years old turned out to be a humiliating defeat for the Arabs.

Three days later, when the engineer observed the tears of joy on the faces of weary Israeli soldiers as they captured the city of Jerusalem, he was struck with the reliability of biblical prophecy. Digging out his old Bible, he opened it to the Gospel of John, which his colleague had earlier suggested to him. When he reached the third chapter, he accepted the reality of God's Word; kneeling alone in his living room, he called on the name of the Lord for salvation. His first profession of his new faith was a three-page letter to me that told this story.

Truly, the fact that the little nation exists today is powerful evidence of the truth that God keeps His promises. The Hebrew prophets were so prolific in their prophecies regarding Israel's destiny that, had there been no reestablishing of the Jews in Palestine in this century, the atheists and skeptics would have had ample reason to consider the Bible discredited. But because the State of Israel is a historical reality, these unbelievers have lapsed into silence on the subject.

The biblical prophecies are too many to enumerate in one chapter. Whole books have been written about them. We will focus our attention instead on several outstanding passages. We have already noted Ezekiel 5:5 in chapter 1 and Amos 9:15 in chapter 3.

Moses the Lawgiver delivered two long statements of prophecy regarding the future of his nation: Leviticus 26:27–45 and Deuteronomy 28:36–68.

Isaiah, one of the greatest Hebrew prophets, dedicated many of his prophecies in chapters 40 through 67 to the themes of Israel's eventual repentance, tribulation, and restoration. These include the way the Messiah will rule from the Promised Land during the kingdom age (or the millennial kingdom), especially in Isaiah 61–62.

One of the lesser-known prophecies is found in Isaiah 19:17–18. This speaks of war between Israel and Egypt in which the Egyptians will be in fear of the Jews, a truth relevant to the wars of 1956 and 1973. One reason why President Sadat of Egypt sought to negotiate for peace with Israel is that he realized his troops were no match for the Jews. However, according to Isaiah 19, these wars would not occur until the Jews were resettled in Palestine. It is a common assumption in the writings of the prophets that Israel would return to the Promised Land.

Jeremiah, another major prophet, provided details concerning Israel's eventual return to the land, and he prophesied,

> "You are saying about this city, 'By the sword, famine and plague it will be handed over to the king of Babylon'; but this is what the LORD, the God of Israel, says: I will surely gather them from all the lands where I banish them in my furious anger and great wrath; I will bring them back to this place and let them live in safety" (Jeremiah 32:36–37).

This is why in our own lifetime millions of Jews have emigrated from many nations to Palestine, either voluntarily or by coercion, and they continue to come.

The third temple

The prophet Daniel and his contemporary Ezekiel both foretold the destruction of the temple in Jerusalem during the Great

Tribulation. Their prophecies obviously do not refer to the temple built by Solomon, for it had already been demolished. Nor do they refer to the second temple, built by Herod, because that was destroyed in A.D. 70 without other aspects of the prophecies being fulfilled. Consequently, these prophecies must speak of a temple still to be built for Jewish worship. This new temple, which will be destroyed by the Antichrist, is alluded to by Jesus (Matthew 24:15), by Paul (2 Thessalonians 2:4), and by John (Revelation 11:3). It is a temple that can be built only at a time when Jews control Jerusalem.

Ezekiel—the specific prophet

Ezekiel makes clear in his prophecies that even though Israel would become dispersed, her people would someday return to the land to make God's holy name known.

> "Therefore say to the house of Israel, 'This is what the Sovereign LORD says: It is not for your sake, O house of Israel, that I am going to do these things, but for the sake of my holy name, which you have profaned among the nations where you have gone. I will show you the holiness of my great name, which has been profaned among the nations, the name you have profaned among them. Then the nations will know that I am the LORD, declares the Sovereign LORD, when I show myself holy through you before their eyes.
>
> " 'For I will take you out of the nations; I will gather you from all the countries and bring you back into your own land. I will sprinkle clean water on you, and you will be clean; I will cleanse you from all your impurities and from your idols. I will give you a new heart and put a new spirit in you; I will remove from you your heart of stone and give you a heart of flesh. And I will put my Spirit in you and move you to follow my decrees and be careful to keep my laws. You will live in the land I gave your forefathers; you will be my people, and I will be your God. I will save you from all your uncleanness. I will call for the grain and make it plentiful and will not bring famine upon you. I will increase the fruit of the trees and the crops of the field, so that you will no longer suffer disgrace among the nations because of famine. Then you will remember your evil ways and wicked deeds, and you will loathe yourselves for your sins and detestable practices. I want you to know that I am not doing this for your sake, declares the Sovereign LORD. Be ashamed and disgraced for your conduct, O house of Israel!'. . .
>
> "So will the ruined cities be filled with flocks of people. Then they will know that I am the LORD" (Ezekiel 36:22–32, 38).

After this prophecy Ezekiel had a vision (Ezekiel 40–48) that cannot be fulfilled until after the Messiah returns to set up His kingdom. During that time Israel will become the blessing God intended her to be. Israel's destiny is absolutely guaranteed by the Word of God. How she would be gathered into the land and how Russia will attempt to destroy her, leading to her spiritual revival, are subjects for later chapters in this book.

Israel—The Living Graveyard

One of the most incredible biblical prophecies is found in Ezekiel 37–39. So many details and specific names are given that the prophecy defies human origin. Only God could forecast such events 2,500 years before they came to pass. The following fourteen verses are incredibly accurate in describing the events of Israel's present-day restoration:

> The hand of the LORD was upon me, and he brought me out by the Spirit of the LORD and set me in the middle of a valley; it was full of bones. He led me back and forth among them, and I saw a great many bones on the floor of the valley, bones that were very dry. He asked me, "Son of man, can these bones live?"
>
> I said, "O Sovereign LORD, you alone know."
>
> Then he said to me, "Prophesy to these bones and say to them, 'Dry bones, hear the word of the LORD! This is what the Sovereign LORD says to these bones: I will make breath enter you, and you will come to life. I will attach tendons to you and make flesh come upon you and cover you with skin; I will put breath in you, and you will come to life. Then you will know that I am the LORD.' "
>
> So I prophesied as I was commanded. And as I was prophesying, there was a noise, a rattling sound, and the bones came together, bone to bone. I looked, and tendons and flesh appeared on them and skin covered them, but there was no breath in them.
>
> Then he said to me, "Prophesy to the breath; prophesy, son of man, and say to it, 'This is what the Sovereign LORD says: Come from the four winds, O breath, and breathe into these slain, that they may live.' " So I prophesied as he commanded me, and breath entered them; they came to life and stood up on their feet—a vast army.
>
> Then he said to me: "Son of man, these bones are the whole house of Israel. They say, 'Our bones are dried up and our hope is gone; we are cut off.' Therefore prophesy and say to them: 'This is what the Sovereign LORD says: O my people, I am going to open your graves and bring you up from them; I will bring you back to the land of

Israel. Then you, my people, will know that I am the Lord, when I open your graves and bring you up from them. I will put my Spirit in you and you will live, and I will settle you in your own land. Then you will know that I the Lord have spoken, and I have done it, declares the Lord' " (Ezekiel 37:1–14).

Who are the dry bones?

Verse 11 states clearly that the bones represent "the whole house of Israel." For nearly 1,900 years Israel naturally represented "dead bones." All Jews were at the mercy of the host nations wherever they live—England, France, Russia, Poland, Germany, the United States, and elsewhere. They had as much chance of becoming a great nation, humanly speaking, as old cars in the junkyard have of suddenly coming to life as new models.

"So I prophesied!"

After receiving the command of God, Ezekiel obeyed and prophesied to this dry-boned nation scattered over the whole world, saying, "I prophesied!" What were the results?

1. "A noise"
2. "A rattling sound"
3. "Bones came together, bone to bone"
4. "Tendons and flesh appeared"
5. "Skin covered them"
6. "But there was no breath in them"

This prophecy obviously forecast a *gradual* coming together. The body of the Jews was scattered all over the graveyard that contains the bones of other civilizations now dead—the Hittites, Assyrians, Babylonians, Chaldeans, Medo-Persians, Greeks, Romans, and on and on. "The dead bones" of Israel would be different; they would gradually leave the graveyard and once again become a living nation.

The resurrection of Israel in this century was not an instantaneous miracle, but one that occurred gradually over a period of thirty-one years.

The historical fulfillment

"A noise, . . .a rattling sound": The single event most influential in getting the Jews back to Palestine from all over the world was the signing of the Balfour Declaration in 1917. Nothing creates "a noise" and "a rattling sound" more than a war. The prophet had an international view of the scattered bones, and the noise was the First World War.

Moreover, the hidden story behind "the noise" is significant. The late Bible scholar David L. Cooper used to tell a story dating from his young manhood during World War I. By 1916 the war was going adversely for England. She was desperate to find a rapid method of manufacturing TNT and smokeless gunpowder in order to repel the German machine guns and other advanced weapons. A brilliant Jew named Chaim Weizmann invented a formula that made rapid production possible, thus changing the course of the war. In return, Lloyd George, the prime minister of England, told Dr. Weizmann to name his reward. Rejecting personal recompense, Weizmann requested that Palestine be declared the national homeland for the Jewish people. Consequently the Balfour Declaration was drafted and signed on November 2, 1917.

In 1917 there were fewer than 25,000 Jews in Palestine. But now, for the first time, the nation that controlled the land gave official sanction to the scattered Jews to reclaim it. And they did, "bone to bone." "But there was no breath in them."

"Tendons and flesh appeared": The 1920s were just the skeleton. There was no meat on the bones. Little national consciousness existed. The government was British, although some small unions of people and voluntary collectives called *kibbutzim* were established. When the Arabs began to attack the defenseless settlers during the twenties, the settlers marshaled unity and strength to resist a common foe. "But there was no breath in them."

"And skin covered them": This part of the biblical imagery could represent the establishment of Israel as a sovereign state in 1948 and its recognition by the valley of living nations. The skin could well signify the organizational unity of self-government. But still "there was no breath in them."

Israel—not a spiritual nation

The word *breath* used symbolically in Scripture indicates spiritual life. From the time God breathed into Adam's nostrils the breath of life to make him a "living soul," God has been more interested in man's spiritual life than his physical. For the most part mankind is just the opposite. Typically, the regathering of Israel into the land from 1917 to the present has been chiefly a physical, political, and economic experience; little attention has been given to the spiritual aspects. Most of the Jews who inhabit the Promised Land today have no "breath" in them *yet*. That is, they are not committed to God by faith and practice. Those whom I have met are rather secular and humanistic.

Theodor Herzl was an atheist, and the Zionist movement that he founded is not a spiritual organization, but reflects strong humanistic tendencies. In fact, the Zionists in the Israeli government are often at odds with the Orthodox rabbis and other minorities who are more prone to be motivated by the Old Testament.

It is significant, however, that Israel is only "a breath away" from fulfilling Ezekiel's prophecy. And as we shall see, this fulfillment will occur suddenly.

Why the Jews?

It is natural to ask, Why should God select the Jews? They are not the most numerous people in the world, totalling only 18 million today, mostly in Israel, the United States, Europe, and the Soviet Union. Neither are they the most religious, for a visit to the Holy Land will convince any observer of their secular spirit. Even on the Sabbath some modern Israeli cities are marred by religious indifference.

There are two reasons for Israel's divine selection as the Chosen people.

1. For His holy name's sake.

In Ezekiel 36:22 God announces through His prophet, "Therefore say to the house of Israel, 'This is what the Sovereign Lord says: It is not for your sake, O house of Israel, that I am going to do these things, but for the sake of my holy name, which you have profaned among the nations where you have gone.'"

God made a promise to Abraham in Genesis 12:1–3:

> The Lord had said to Abram, "Leave your country, your people and your father's household and go to the land I will show you. I will

make you into a great nation and I will bless you; I will make your name great, and you will be a blessing. I will bless those who bless you, and whoever curses you I will curse; and all peoples on earth will be blessed through you."

Later God reaffirmed this covenant with Abraham, as recorded in Genesis 15:4–6, 18. God keeps His Word; therefore we can expect Israel to be in the land of Palestine when the Messiah, Jesus Christ, returns. Even the American Zionist Council accepts this promise. Despite its secularity, the New York branch of the council was quoted as saying, after 1.5 million Jews had returned to the land in only fifteen years, "Return from exile has taken on a swiftness of tempo and greatness of scale that carries the mind back to the mighty soaring prophecies of the Bible." The Zionists then quoted several biblical prophecies:

"I will bring you from the nations and gather you from the countries where you have been scattered—with a mighty hand and an outstretched arm and with outpoured wrath" (Ezekiel 20:34).

"See, they will come from afar—some from the north, some from the west, some from the region of Sinim [Aswan]." Shout for joy, O heavens; rejoice, O earth; burst into song, O mountains! For the LORD comforts his people and will have compassion on his afflicted ones (Isaiah 49:12–13).

2. God's plan for mankind

God performed a biological miracle when Abraham and Sarah were beyond the age of child-bearing in order to bring into this world a special people. He intended them to be His "torchbearers," or communicators of His Word. Those who have obeyed Him—like the prophets, good kings, judges—have been the "blessing" He promised. Those who have opposed Him have often been a hindrance to mankind. But before this world ends, God will yet use Jews in a very special way as messengers of His gospel of grace.

From a biblical perspective, God is not through with Israel. The Jews are still to be "His people" who fearlessly share His message of salvation with a lost world—much as did the first-century apostles, who were all Jews.

The prophet Joel foretold,

Then the LORD will be jealous for his land and take pity on his people. The LORD will reply to them: "I am sending you grain, new

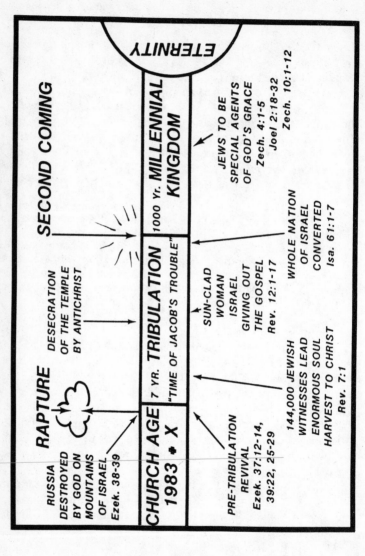

GOD'S PLAN FOR THE FUTURE

SECOND COMING

RAPTURE

DESECRATION
OF THE TEMPLE
BY ANTICHRIST

RUSSIA
DESTROYED
BY GOD ON
MOUNTAINS
OF ISRAEL
Ezek. 38-39

CHURCH AGE 7 YR. TRIBULATION 1000 Yr. MILLENNIAL KINGDOM
1983 • X   "TIME OF JACOB'S TROUBLE"

ETERNITY

JEWS TO BE
SPECIAL AGENTS
OF GOD'S GRACE
Zech. 4:1-5
Joel 2:18-32   Zech. 10:1-12

WHOLE NATION
OF ISRAEL
CONVERTED
Isa. 61:1-7

SUN-CLAD
WOMAN
ISRAEL
GIVING OUT
THE GOSPEL
Rev. 12:1-17

144,000 JEWISH
WITNESSES LEAD
ENORMOUS SOUL
HARVEST TO CHRIST
Rev. 7:1

PRE-TRIBULATION
REVIVAL
Ezek. 37:12-14,
39:22, 25-29

wine and oil, enough to satisfy you fully; never again will I make you an object of scorn to the nations" (Joel 2:18–19).

"I will repay you for the years the locusts have eaten—the great locust and the young locust, the other locusts and the locust swarm—my great army that I send among you. You will have plenty to eat, until you are full, and you will praise the name of the LORD your God, who has worked wonders for you; never again will my people be shamed. Then you will know that I am in Israel, that I am the LORD your God, and that there is no other; never again will my people be shamed.

"And afterward, I will pour out my Spirit on all people. Your sons and daughters will prophesy, your old men will dream dreams, your young men will see visions. Even on my servants, both men and women, I will pour out my Spirit in those days. I will show wonders in the heavens and on the earth, blood and fire and billows of smoke. The sun will be turned to darkness and the moon to blood before the coming of the great and dreadful day of the LORD. And everyone who calls on the name of the LORD will be saved; for on Mount Zion and in Jerusalem there will be deliverance, as the LORD has said, among the survivors whom the LORD calls" (Joel 2:25–32).

The Next Step

Unlike other nations, Israel has a guaranteed future. Many Bible teachers believe that the current regathering of the Jews into the land and the establishment of statehood are part of God's fulfilling His plan.

As we shall see, many trials and joys yet await this young nation before *all* God's promises will be fulfilled. There may be some minor setbacks ahead. But a time of "peace and safety" will come, to be followed by a vicious attack from Russia and her hordes, before God supernaturally interferes with the affairs of nations to spare Israel in terms that all the world will understand.

This earth has some exciting days ahead, and one of the most unbelievable is the coming peace in the Middle East.

5.　The Coming Peace Treaty

The event most unreasonable to predict for the Middle East is a peace treaty between the Arabs and the Jews. But that is exactly what I anticipate, and I expect it to come to pass *before* Russia invades Israel and before the United States and Russia enter into a nuclear holocaust. It may happen before the tribulation is over, and even before the rapture of the church.

The hatred engulfing the Jews, the Arabs, and the homeless Palestinians grows worse day by day. The ancient hostilities and the conflicting religious beliefs among these peoples have only been intensified by the recent warfare among them in Lebanon. Consider the "impossible" circumstances that make a peace treaty a dim hope from a human perspective.

Why Peace Seems Remote

1. Jewish control of Jerusalem

Jerusalem and the temple site are now controlled by the Jews. The government of Israel allows the Arabs free access to the Dome of the Rock, the second most holy site in Islam, and the El-Aqsa mosque. But it is extremely aggravating to the Arabs to find Jewish soldiers in the city, controlling access.

2. The West Bank

The Jews are continually developing settlements in the West Bank region that was designated by the United Nations for Palestinians, but rejected by the latter. Their safety guaranteed by Israeli troops, the settlers construct permanent dwellings for their growing population—a sign to the Palestinians that the Jews have no intention of surrendering this territory.

3. Growing Israeli arrogance

After five wars and hundreds of skirmishes, the Jews recognize that the Arabs are no match for them, regardless of their vastly greater numbers. While some Jews in the military and in civilian life acknowledge the hand of God in their victories, many respond with a spirit of superiority. Centuries ago the children of Israel were overawed by the Canaanites and exclaimed, "We are as grasshoppers in their sight." Now many Arabs see themselves as inferior soldiers, and it infuriates them.

4. Warfare in Lebanon

Syrian military setbacks and the evacuation by the Palestine Liberation Organization as a result of Israel's invasion of Lebanon in 1982 have only served to harden Arab determination, motivated by vengeance and national honor.

5. Unstable government in Lebanon

The unwelcome presence of the PLO increased internal strife after civil war broke out in Lebanon in 1975. Though the PLO is gone, the country remains at war, with the power struggle among Muslims, Christians, and Druze taking a steady toll politically and physically.

6. The PLO power struggle

Yasir Arafat, chairman of the PLO, is fighting to retain leadership, against extremist elements who believe he is not aggressive enough in the Palestinian cause. No matter who wins, the result will be greater antagonism against Israel by the PLO, not less.

7. Annexation of the Golan Heights

Syria has never forgiven Israel for capturing the Golan Heights near the Sea of Galilee in the Six-Day War of 1967. Now that Israel has annexed it permanently, the Syrians are incensed.

8. *Syria's occupation of Lebanon*

Syria wants control of Lebanon, which the former still considers part of "Greater Syria." The only real obstacles to their fulfilling this goal are Israel's military presence and diplomatic pressure from the United States.

9. *The cost of keeping troops in Lebanon*

Neither Israel nor Syria can afford to keep thousands of soldiers on duty in Lebanon indefinitely without a heavy drain on their national economies. They cannot play a waiting game for long, but will have to resort to aggressive action to resolve the conflict.

10. *The destabilizing influence of Russia*

Left to themselves, the Arabs have proved to be no match for the Jews. In all their wars they have relied on armaments from the Soviet Union or other Communist nations. In some cases, Arab countries not adjacent to Israel—such as Saudi Arabia or Iraq— have supplied the arms or dollars needed to foment war; but the hand of Russia has never been far removed.

While the Russians have forfeited much money and equipment in the Middle East conflicts, they have gained influence and Arab dependency. Communism's basic atheism is diametrically opposed to Muslim theism, making most Arab countries anti-Communist. But the Arabs' excessive hatred for the Jews has forced them to become dependent on the Communists to advance their own ends.

War often makes strange bedfellows. I believe that ultimately the Arab nations will become Russian satellites. Indeed, despite Arab setbacks during the fighting in Lebanon in 1982, the Communists quickly began to rearm Arab countries, particularly Syria and Egypt.

11. *Arab jealousy over Israel's economic success*

Israel is not a rich country—yet. No nation could immigrate six times its population in the space of thirty-five years and grow rich. The inflation rate is high, due largely to disproportionate spending for national defense—which it views pragmatically as the price of retaining freedom. In spite of this, the economy of Israel far outdistances that of the average Arab nation (in part because of heavy investments for industrialization by Jews in

Europe and America), and her standard of living is higher as well—a thorn in the side of the less-developed Arab nations.

Where Will It End?

The logical conclusion to all these conditions is a war in the Middle East to end all wars. And according to biblical prophecy, it will happen—but not for some time. Before that a peace treaty will put a stop to the terrorism, the fighting, the fear, and the human suffering of both sides. Both the Arabs and Israel will temporarily enjoy safety and harmony. For the Jews, at least, it will be an era of unprecedented economic prosperity.

Some 2,500 years ago the prophet Ezekiel declared that peace and prosperity would come to Israel *before* Russia invades her country.

> "Get ready; be prepared, you and all the hordes gathered about you, and take command of them. After many days you will be called to arms. In future years you will invade a land that has recovered from war, whose people were gathered from many nations to the mountains of Israel, which had long been desolate. They had been brought out from the nations, and now *all of them live in safety"* (Ezekiel 38:7–8).

> "This is what the Sovereign LORD says: On that day thoughts will come into your mind and you will devise an evil scheme. You will say, 'I will invade a land of *unwalled villages;* I will attack *a peaceful and unsuspecting people—all of them living without walls and without gates and bars*. I will plunder and loot and turn my hand against the resettled ruins and the people gathered from the nations, rich in livestock and goods, living at the center of the land' " (Ezekiel 38:10–12, author's italics).

The invader of Israel, as we shall see, will be Russia. But notice the condition of Israel before Russia launches her attack. Israel is a land "recovered from war" and "gathered from many nations to the mountains of Israel." Yet they all "live in safety" as "a peaceful and unsuspecting people . . . without walls and without gates and bars."

But to this day Israel has never enjoyed these conditions. No Jew in Palestine has truly been secure and safe from the time of the first Arab attacks on Jewish settlements in 1929. Once the Israeli government exhausted the patience of the United Nations by presenting a documented list of more than one thousand attacks on its people or cities by Arab terrorists. Ever since they entered the land, their national defense has been in a state of readiness.

What Does It All Mean?

As impossible as it seems, there must somehow be a settlement in the Middle East to enable the Jews to live at peace in the land. And it cannot be a false peace without rational assurances. As weary of war and insecurity as the Jews may be, they are not about to surrender their land or believe easy political promises from the United Nations. Yet the prophet affirmed that they would be "unsuspecting" (which may not apply to the Mossad, Israel's crack intelligence organization).

The peace treaty will provide safety when Israel's defenses are down, but it will be enforced long enough for the nation to become "rich in livestock and goods.' If three million inhabitants directed their ingenuity totally toward tilling the land, producing, inventing, and providing services instead of toward warfare, Israel could become a rich land in a very few years. Such great prosperity would evoke greed from Russia. But on the basis of my observations on visits to Israel, I believe she will have to become much richer than she is now to draw that attraction from the Soviet Union.

This condition may suggest that Israel is in for an economic bonanza. It could be the discovery of a gigantic oil field, a rare and valuable mineral, or some way to export the seemingly inexhaustible supply of mineral deposits in the Dead Sea. For some reason God located Israel in "the center of the earth," where discoveries can quickly change her present economic condition.

The Coming Middle East Peace

The prophetic affirmation of a peace treaty has not been lost on other Bible teachers. It is suggested in the book *Armageddon, Oil and the Middle East Crisis* by John F. and John E. Walvoord.

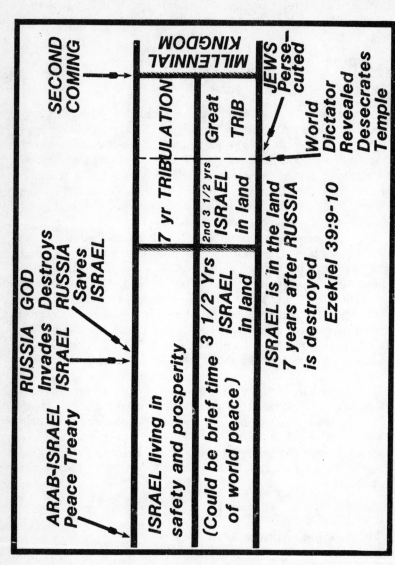

ARAB-ISRAEL Peace Treaty

RUSSIA GOD
Invades Destroys
ISRAEL RUSSIA
Saves
ISRAEL

SECOND COMING

MILLENNIAL KINGDOM

7 yr TRIBULATION

Great TRIB

JEWS Perse—cuted

World Dictator Revealed Desecrates Temple

ISRAEL living in safety and prosperity

(Could be brief time of world peace)

3 1/2 Yrs ISRAEL in land

2nd 3 1/2 yrs ISRAEL in land

ISRAEL is in the land 7 years after RUSSIA is destroyed Ezekiel 39:9-10

A brief world peace

Admittedly, they place the peace treaty at the first part of the Tribulation, a view I do not accept. Yet their comments are worthy of our consideration.

> All signs point to the necessity of a coming peace settlement in the Middle East. The industrialized nations cannot continue to tolerate the disruption of oil supplies in the world market. The struggles between Israel and the Arab nations cannot continue to push the entire world repeatedly to the brink of nuclear war.
>
> The overwhelming weight of population advantage, proximity to Russia as a supplier of arms, and the tremendous power of the oil blackmail give the Arab world the ultimate advantage at the peace table. In Israel, changing internal politics may demand some mobilization of the military and dependence on outside guarantees for Israel's security. The United States will be reluctant to give such guarantees which might cause another military involvement overseas. The international political leader who can give Israel these guarantees and force dissident Arab factions to accept a final peace will gain world recognition overnight.[1]

I will show that Russia must be destroyed *at least* three and one-half years before the Tribulation. Therefore, this era of peace must precede that period of seven years.

This world wants peace more than anything else—a peace that brings prosperity. The United Nations was founded for the purpose of insuring peace, but typical of mankind's attempts to solve its problems independent of God, the organization has been a failure. More wars have been fought since the founding of the U.N. in 1945 than in any comparable span of years in history. It will not be the means for gaining this Israeli peace.

Rather, it is possibly because of the oil resources that a peace treaty might be secured among the Western powers and Russia. But if such a treaty were to take effect in the Middle East, it would be short-lived.

Peace Treaty? How?

The prophet Ezekiel was specifically instructed by God to say to "Gog,"

---

[1]John F. Walvoord and John E. Walvoord, *Armageddon, Oil and the Middle East Crisis* (Grand Rapids: Zondervan, 1974, rev. ed. 1976), 113.

"This is what the Sovereign LORD says: In that day, when my
people Israel are living in safety, will you not take notice of it? You
will come from your place in the far north, you and many nations with
you. . ." (Ezekiel 38:14–15)

We will see in a later chapter that this nation from *the north* can
only be Russia, and "Gog" signifies her head of state. Moreover,
the time of peace will occur at least three and one-half years
before the tribulation period. There will actually be two peace
treaties: the one we are discussing which will provide time for
Israel to become so prosperous that Russia will want to attack
her *personally,* and the one foretold by the prophet Daniel
(9:27) between the Antichrist and Israel that will officially start
the tribulation period.

What possible event or world conditions could occur to bring
about such a peace in Palestine? No one knows, but we might
speculate on some possibilities. These are only *possible* conditions in an imagined scenario.

1. If Russia stops arming the Arabs

The Arabs cannot offer a threat to Israel if Russia or other
Communist countries do not supply them with the weapons of
war. Israel is already armed to the teeth with the latest U.S.
weaponry and an enormous cache of materiel captured in
Lebanon in 1982. Fortunately, the Russian equipment— particularly the rocketry—has proved to be inferior and the Arabs
inadequately trained to use it. But without this military hard-
ware, the Arabs would be at the mercy of Israel and forced into a
negotiated peace. If somehow Russia could be expelled from
Middle East manipulations, such a peace would come naturally,
for on their own turf Israel's might is awesome. The Arabs
without Russian aid are impotent.

2. A Russo-American arms treaty (Salt III).

There is great worldwide sympathy for a nuclear or conventional
arms treaty between the superpowers. Russia's world expansion-
ist activities during the past fifty years have taken an enormous
toll on the economy of her country—far worse than the role of
world policeman has taken on the United States.

Even a U.S. president with a "hardline" foreign policy toward
the Soviet Union could be enticed to negotiate an arms treaty by

Communist wiles. Suppose their negotiations went a step further to produce an agreement to stop their supply of arms to friends in the Middle East. Such an event would assure Israel of the peace and safety ·the prophet Ezekiel predicted. It could force the misplaced Palestinians to accept living in the West Bank or even to agree on another homeland not yet considered. The fact is, neither the United Nations nor the two superpowers are dealing conclusively with the question of a homeland for Palestinians.

I am convinced of this, however: if Russia and the United States negotiate a treaty that guarantees peace in the Middle East, they can force both Arabs and Jews to accept it.

3. A worldwide economic collapse and depression

Knowledgeable economists have been sounding the warning that the world's entire monetary system is on the brink of collapse. So many countries owe more money to the world bank than they can pay that the International Monetary Fund is in danger of failure unless subsidized by the American taxpayer. Poland, Brazil, and Mexico have all publicly threatened to default on their loans. So far the bankers have put together a "financial package" to rescue these defaulting countries—a euphemism for "rolling over the debt" or paying interest on interest.

Someday this monetary house of cards must collapse, and when it does, the chain reaction in every country will bring industrial growth and economic systems to a halt, producing a worldwide depression even more disastrous than the great depression of the thirties. Such an economic collapse could create such pressure that the Jews and Arabs, no longer backed by the wealth of the United States and Russia, would be forced to sign a peace treaty.

Out of the ruins of such an economic collapse, Israel could somehow refurbish its economy and begin to prosper until she became the object of greed and plunder for Russia in the last days. Such earth-shaking events are very possible; under present conditions they could appear on the world scene very soon.

4. A "scorched earth" attack by Israel

The patience of Israel's leaders is wearing thin. They know that if there is to be an end to the terrorist attacks or wars that have plagued them ever since they established their nation, it will probably have to be by force: theirs. While Western arms will continue to be available, the Israelis don't expect that land troops from Western countries will ever be deployed in the Middle East.

Consequently, Israel may launch an all-out attack on the PLO or its successor someday, chasing the foe all the way to the northern borders of Lebanon, Syria, and Jordan. The Israelis could even decide to take over the governments in those countries or, like the Communists, establish puppet governments. While that is an unlikely occurrence, it would not be so surprising for the Israeli military command to be given a scorched-earth policy against the PLO or its Arab successors—that is, a policy of destroying anything that has military and strategic value to the enemy.

While the nations of the world would raise a protest and "sanctions" would be leveled against Israel by the United Nations, little if any real action would result. Even Russia—preoccupied with Afghanistan, Cuba, and her Eastern European satellites—would do little more than protest. Saudi Arabia, Iraq, Iran, and other Middle Eastern nations would do nothing more. One diplomat put it, "What good is a giant marshmallow at a time of war?" This scenario remains one of the most probable toward the coming peace treaty, especially since there could soon be a more aggressive leader than Yasir Arafat in the PLO.

5. A glut of world oil

The high inflation that plagued the world in the late seventies and early eighties, resulting in skyrocketing oil prices, caused a cutback in gasoline use as high as 25 percent in some countries. This, together with the discovery of new oil fields, has caused a glut of oil that—if permitted to continue—could further weaken the Arab nations economically. If energy conservation continues, oil prices could decline significantly. This would decrease the Arabs' ability to oppose Israel militarily and compel the archenemies to negotiate for peace. This in turn would have the following effects:

- Force the Arabs to recognize Israel and deal with her as a sovereign state;
- Solve the Palestinian problem with fairness and justice;

- Guarantee free access to Jerusalem;
- Enable Israelis to live in their land with security.

6. *The discovery of oil in Palestine*

Suppose that a pool of oil, greater than anything in Arabia, Alaska, or the Falkland Islands, were discovered by the Jews in Palestine. This would change the course of history. Before long, Israel would be able independently to solve its economic woes, finance the resettlement of the Palestinians, and supply housing for Jews and Arabs in the West Bank, East Bank, or anywhere else they might choose to live.

Even if something besides oil were discovered, it would have the same far-reaching effect if it were able to produce high revenues.

7. *An Arab-Israeli religious truce*

The most unlikely possibility leading to peace is a religious truce. I believe nothing short of military force can solve the dispute over who owns the Dome of the Rock. Both Arabs and Jews venerate the site as a holy place—the Arabs, because it is traditionally held to be the place where Abraham was prepared to offer his son Isaac as a sacrifice; and the Jews, because it is considered the central location of Solomon's temple. The temple is going to be rebuilt, according to biblical prophecy, so the religious significance of the site will not diminish, nor will its political implications.

It has been suggested that Jewish archaeologists have discovered that Solomon's temple was not built over the rock covered by the Muslim mosque, but was situated several hundred feet to the north. If this should prove to be true, it offers the possibility that the new temple could be built without disturbing that Muslim holy site. This could provide the basis for a religious truce.

I believe, however, that such a truce would have to carry with it reparations for the Palestinians. Although at this time Israel cannot afford to pay reparations, the world's bankers and the major countries have so much to gain by a peace treaty in the Middle East that it would be to their advantage to contribute to such a fund.

During a recent tour of the Holy Land, Dr. Arthur Peters—

then president of Christian Heritage College—asked his Arab guide, "Who do you think the land of Palestine belongs to?" Amazingly the guide replied, "I realize that the scriptures promise the land to Israel and that it will belong to them when the Lord Jesus Christ returns to this earth in His second coming. But in the meantime, they should share the land with us!" Admittedly this guide was a born-again Christian and did not reflect the thinking of all Palestinians, but he does represent the thinking of most fair-minded people. Even many Jews believe that the Arabs and Jews can share the land. Any peace treaty that provides safety and security to Israel will have to include adequate provisions for the Arabs.

Dr. Louis Goldberg, a well-known Bible scholar, suggests a view he calls the "the Two State reality," a position held as well by many Israelis of the Alignment party. Its proponents advocate, alongside the State of Israel, a union of the West Bank and Gaza Strip with the Kingdom of Jordan. With minor variations, many in the Alignment camp support a position set forth by former Prime Minister Yitzhak Rabin in his memoirs.[2] Rabin points out that 90 percent of all Palestinian Arabs live in the West Bank, Gaza Strip, and the State of Jordan. For this reason, he argues, it would be most natural to forge these territories into a single state. He feels this is the most viable solution to the problem as long as Israel's borders are guaranteed.

8. A natural disaster

A geological or meteorological event could remarkably change the topography to such a degree that many of the existing economic and political conditions would no longer fuel the tensions. Weather conditions, earthquakes, and volcanic activity are bringing frightening changes to much of the earth's surface and her inhabitants. Suppose an upheaval occurred that carved a channel like the Red Sea from the Mediterranean through the Dead Sea. And what if it turned the Sinai or another desert area into livable real estate? Such a phenomenon could help to effect a peace treaty.

---

[2]Yitzhak Rabin, *The Rabin Memoirs* (Boston: Little, Brown, 1979).

9. *None of the above*

It is possible, of course, that the decisive factor leading to a peace treaty between Arabs and Jews is not included in any of these eight scenarios. Or it might be a combination of these events.

But of this I am certain: Israel will enjoy tranquillity in the land before Russia sweeps down to take her captive. Israel will probably make a peace treaty not only with the Arab nations, but also with the Russians. Without Russia's cooperation in a peace initiative, there will be no peace. Yet we should not be surprised when Russia eventually breaks the treaty. The Russians have already violated fifty-two such treaties. This philosophy of utilitarianism and deceit will cause them to totally disregard this treaty once it is established, but only after it has provided unprecedented peace and prosperity to Israel and possibly other parts of the Middle East.

Biblical prophecy makes it clear that, like it or not, Russia will always be a factor to contend with in the Middle East puzzle.

6. Russia—The Thorn in the World's Side

"This is what the Sovereign LORD says: I am against you, O Gog, chief prince of Meshech and Tubal. . ." (Ezekiel 38:3).

The Communist government of Russia is the most evil government in the history of mankind. Measured by the number of deaths it has caused, by the peace it has stolen, the suffering it has created, the people it has enslaved, and the dreams and human aspirations it has shattered, it is judged worse than the empires of Adolf Hitler, Kaiser Wilhelm, Napoleon Bonaparte, Genghis Khan, and Muhammad combined.

A study on global violence prepared by the Center for Defense Information in Washington, D.C., reveals that more than five million lives were lost during 1983 in the forty countries that have experienced outright war or some form of revolutionary insurgencies.[1] Communist agitation was a factor in 80 percent of the trouble spots.

From Afghanistan—where 105,000 Russian troops are seeking to impose communism—to Central America and Africa, Russia and her Communist agitators are stirring up strife. Every year millions of innocent lives are added to the debt the Communists owe God and humanity. Russian communism is easily the most pernicious form of government ever conceived.

The Soviets claim to be a government of the common people, but nothing can be further from the truth. Almost seventy years of Communist rule in Russia proves that the quality of human life has not improved for her people; it is stifled. As a form of

---

[1] 'A World at War—1983,' quoted in *U.S. News and World Report* (July 11, 1983):44–45.

government, communism merely represents a change in leadership from elitists of the czar's family to elitists of the Communists. Their political format is always the same. They stir up local strife in the name of "liberation," then take over by force and establish their brand of totalitarianism. In Cuba the government shifted from elitist Baptista and dictatorship to elitist Castro and terrorism. Only one consistent trend can be traced in the many Communist takeovers since 1917: the Communist government is always worse than the one it replaces, as measured by personal freedom, free elections, or economic stability.

But the real story lies in the death toll effected by Communist dictators once they assume control. Whether in Russia—where at least 37 million lives have been exterminated since the Communist revolution of 1917—or in China—where the toll is 67 million since 1949—it is ever the same. Communism is the most brutally totalitarian form of government known to man, and only the intellectual idealists in our educational system, in government, and in the media fail to recognize it. They will not listen to the Russian intellectual and exiled author, Alexsandr Solzhenitsyn, who spent many years imprisoned in the *gulag*—the labor camps of Siberia.

Russian Leaders Are Murderers

One of the notorious blindspots of the secular humanists who would be our national spokesmen and leaders is the belief that government leaders of nondemocratic countries are honorable people. They fail to understand the nature of communism, which is built on the principle of "the survival of the fittest." Joseph Stalin succeeded Lenin, not because he was a better administrator or loved by the people, but because he was the most ruthless of the Communist ruling elite. The historical record tells us that he was a butcher who cruelly disposed of anyone who stood in his way. The testimony of his contemporaries echoes this judgment.

Dr. Louis S. Bauman, a Bible scholar, wrote in 1935, "G. Bessyedovsky, former Soviet Ambassador to Paris, says of Stalin. . .he has the characteristics of an Asiatic satrap who tolerates no obstacles in his path. When his old friend Kamo, with whom he organized armed raids on banks in the days of Czarism, was recently run over by an automobile in Tiflis, Stalin, in wrath, sent a telegram to the Tiflis OGPU. 'Shoot the driver at once.' Although the driver was not at fault, and although he was also a Communist, he was shot without trial. When Pyatakov, a noted Communist, fell seriously ill from the excess of drinking, Stalin, beside himself with anger, called the physicians and ordered them: 'Cure him in two weeks!' *And Pyatakov was cured!''* [2]

The idealist will respond, "But that was long ago. Today's Russians are much more humanitarian." Yet the late Yuri Andropov, Soviet president from 1982 to 1984, headed the KGB—the Russian secret police—for fifteen years. The KGB is the most autocratic and powerful single organization in the world. It is answerable to no one; it is feared by all, especially the citizens of the Soviet Union themselves. Was its former leader worthy of trust simply because he became the elitist leader of the Soviets?

In September 1983 a Korean civilian passenger jet, Flight 007, was shot down by Soviet MiG fighter planes, killing 269 people, including my good friend, U.S. Representative Larry MacDonald. President Reagan rightly called it an act of barbarism. The Russians could well have staged the entire event; they have the ability to scramble the guidance system of an aircraft and could easily have led the plane off course. I am convinced that they knew that Dr. MacDonald, the strongest anti-Communist among the elected members of the United States government, was on that plane. They are fully capable of deliberately massacring 268 others because they wanted to kill him. The Communists have shown comparable disregard for human life in the past.

Every week major periodicals in the United States recount gruesome details of Communist infiltration and attempts to take over Central America and forcibly impose a Soviet Castro-style government on its innocent people. Literally millions of people have lost their lives, their homes, or their jobs, and they will never again be the same because of the vicious desire for conquest on the part of the Russians. If the Russians are successful, it will only be a matter of time until the United States

---

[2]Louis S. Bauman, *Light From Biblical Prophecy* (New York: Fleming H. Revell, 1935), 40.

is flooded with illegal aliens, and the Communists will immediately move to take over South America before turning toward the United States herself. God is against Gog because Russia is against people.

Why Single Out the Russians?

Next to His Son, human beings are dearest to the heart of God. He seems to love them even more than He does the angels, for He sent His only begotten Son to die for mankind. Only mankind can sin against God, yet be forgiven and granted eternal life through belief in His Son.

Yet, in two chapters of the Book of Ezekiel, God establishes that He is *against* the nation of Russia. That is most unusual, because history shows that God is *for* mankind. There must be some compelling reason why God, who loves mankind so much that He gave His Son for us, would turn so aggressively against an entire nation. The key, I believe, is the satanic presence that indwells the Russian leaders. In several Old Testament prophecies, God's proclamation of judgment went far beyond the immediate kingdom to the spirit of Satan that controlled the rulers.

The power of government to oppress billions of people was never lost on Satan. Early in human history he learned to give special attention to world leaders—as he will to the Antichrist world dictator during the tribulation period. For if Satan controls the dictator, king, or leader of a country, he will ultimately tyrannize that country. In Daniel's day the supreme example was Nebuchadnezzar. Satan exercised dominion over both king and country; thus God opposed both the nation of Babylon, because of its unrighteous ways, and the spirit of Satan, which indwelt the king.

So it is with Russia. God not only abhors Russia but the source of power behind it, Satan himself. Consider these prophecies from a loving God who declares He is *against* Russia, her leader, her capital city, and one of her major provinces.

> The word of the LORD came to me: "Son of man, set your face against Gog, of the land of Magog, the chief prince of Meshech and Tubal; prophesy against him and say: 'This is what the Sovereign

LORD says: I am against you, O Gog, chief prince of Meshech and Tubal' " (Ezekiel 38:1-3).

"Son of man, prophesy against Gog and say: 'This is what the Sovereign LORD says: I am against you, O Gog, chief prince of Meshech and Tubal. I will turn you around and drag you along. I will bring you from the far north and send you against the mountains of Israel. Then I will strike your bow from your left hand and make your arrows drop from your right hand' " (Ezekiel 39:1-3).

God not only opposes Russia, but vividly describes her coming destruction, vowing, "I will give you as food to all kinds of carrion birds and to the wild animals" (Ezekiel 39:4). This is similar to our Lord's prediction concerning the armies of the Antichrist (Matthew 24:28; Revelation 19:17-21). Such graphic prophecies are reserved not just for Stalinlike dictators who brutalize their subjects, but the Satanic spirit that indwells them. This judgment is really aimed at the Satanic power within "Gog," the chief ruler of the Russians.

God Against Gog

Ever since the Bolshevik Revolution, Satan has ostensibly made his antihuman headquarters the city of Moscow and his personal dwelling such leaders of the nation as Lenin, Stalin, Khrushchev, Brezhnev, and Andropov. Under Satanic influence they have incited communism's antihuman governmental systems to enslave upward of 1.5 billion people and have incurred the wrath of God for three reasons:

1. They have propagated an atheistic religion.

The most heinous sin in God's eyes is to deceive people by teaching a religion other than the gospel of Christ. Our Lord revealed the attitude of God in every deed. He always had time for repentant sinners and showered mercy upon them. He reserved His severest strictures, not for adulterers, tax collectors, or other sinners, but for the religious leaders of His day. Why? They had deceived people about God.

The doctrine of atheism is such an integral part of communism that wherever the philosophy has gone—either in a totalitarian takeover of a country or in the infiltration of the universities of the free world—its teachers have always taught materialism and atheism, the fundamental doctrines of Karl Marx and his disciples. They have appealed to the masses with their philosophy of economic socialism, because it attracts votes. An irony of history is that the precepts of communism have never worked successfully. Never has communism raised the standard of living in any country. In addition, every country that has voted Communists into power in a free election has always voted them out of power at the first opportunity.

Since its inception, communism has consistently fostered a rejection of God, supplanting Him with a belief in "man's potential, not God's." It is safe to say that no other philosophy of life has created more skeptics, agnostics, and unbelievers.

Communism has been effective in polluting the minds of young people in the Western world because it is so close to secular humanism. This philosophy of life, to one degree or another, is held by most of those who occupy chairs of philosophy, law, or education in the major universities and other educational institutions of the West. As I have explained in my four books on secular humanism, not all secular humanists are Communists, but all Communists are secular humanists.[3] Therefore it would be easy for Communists to infiltrate educational institutions in any country, even in the free world. Posing as secular humanists, they teach their anti-God, anti-morality, anti-free enterprise, and anti-Christianity philosophy. Many Communists have used this subterfuge to earn their living at taxpayers' expense in our educational institutions, spending their entire lifetimes polluting the faith of as many of the 13 million college students in America as they can. Of course, they pursue the same ends throughout the rest of the Western world.

I debated one secular humanist who has been a philosophy professor in a major educational institution on the West Coast for forty years. He proudly testified that he had changed the faith of many of his students who came from "fundamentalist Christian homes." I do not know whether the man is a Communist, but it really doesn't matter. The shocking effects on his students are the same whether he is or isn't.

---

[3]*The Battle for the Mind* (1980); *The Battle for the Public Schools* (1982); *The Battle for the Public Schools* (1983); *The Hidden Censors* (1984), all published by Fleming H. Revell, Old Tappan, N.J.

The great tragedy in all of this is that young people do not become unbelievers because of lack of evidence. God has supplied overwhelming testimony in the Bible regarding His existence, His supernaturalness, and the supernaturalness of Jesus Christ. I have had the joy of leading many people to Christ after they have thoroughly investigated the logical reasons for accepting the bodily resurrection of Jesus as historical fact. Why, then, in the face of persuasive evidence, do so many young people become unbelievers in our secular institutions? It is simply that the evidence is not taught in those institutions. Consequently young people become atheists or agnostics after examining only one side of the issue—the infidel's side.

Most college professors believe that their anti-God position is the only one entitled to exposure in the halls of academia. When one contemplates the infiltrated universities of the Western world, the physically dominated universities of the Communist world, and the many other places that Communists and humanist sympathizers have penetrated with their educational missionary work, it is probably safe to say that Russia has damned as many souls intellectually as she has destroyed physically. No wonder God says, "I am against you, O Gog."

2. Russia has violated more biblical principles than any other nation.

The Soviet Union continually teaches people to act as she does. It is one thing to blatantly teach atheism; it is another to infuse a lifestyle that is diametrically opposed to the purposes of God.

The Bible makes it clear that happiness is the result of obeying God's principles (Luke 11:28). We are seeing this vividly illustrated in the social and family scene in the United States today. The Christian families who practice biblical principles enjoy harmony and love in an openly anti-Christian culture. By contrast, those who follow the philosophy of secular humanism and communism—man as the center of all things, and self-indulgence, self-actualization, and self-realization as his primary purpose—seriously compound their difficulties.

It is one of the longstanding tactics of Communists to pollute the morals of a nation they have targeted for takeover. They successfully assaulted the morals of Great Britain before and during World War II, then came to Canada and America to duplicate the process during the past three decades. For example, who has advocated "free love," "permissive sex, " "abortion on demand," "homosexual rights," "the free distribution of pornography," and "the removal of laws against nonprescriptive drugs and marijuana"? It has not been parents, church leaders, construction workers, or family-oriented people. These radical social activities have been consistently advocated from the halls of our prestigious universities and colleges, where secular humanist and Communist teachings are welcomed with open arms.

As an active opponent of the radical kind of sex education in mixed classes that has proliferated over the past two decades, I have documentation that this teaching emanated from the World Health Organization (WHO) and the United Nations Educational, Scientific and Cultural Organization (UNESCO). What better way to pollute the morals of a nation than to have teachers create an obsession with sex in the minds of our young? First they tell them how to do it, then they permit Planned Parenthood to enter the schools and provide contraceptives to avert the consequences of promiscuity.

Nevertheless, the judgment of God has fallen on America and on the rest of the world where such practices are advocated. Twenty-one million sexually promiscuous individuals are carriers of the incurable disease "herpes." People who practice chastity, morality, and sexual fidelity with a lifetime mate, as the Bible teaches, do not face that problem. But the spread of the disease weakens the moral fabric of a nation and benefits the Communist plans for encirclement of the Americas.

Another evidence of the judgment of God appears in the AIDS (Anti-Immunity Deficiency Syndrome) epidemic that has resulted from widespread homosexuality. Who has encouraged this lifestyle? Secular humanists and Communist professors on college and university campuses in America.

If Jesus were on earth today, He would say of the Communists what he said of the Pharisees in Matthew 23:15–16:

> You travel over land and sea to win a single convert, and when he becomes one, you make him twice as much a son of hell as you are. Woe to you, blind guides!

God is against Russia because of its soul-damning philosophy of atheism.

3. Russia has persecuted the Jews.

Everyone knows that Karl Marx was a Jew, and most people realize that both Lenin and Stalin were partially Jewish. But many do not realize that the majority of the leading fifty men who seized control of Russia in the Bolshevik Revolution were also Jews.

Since then, however, there has been a systematic purge of Jewish leadership within the Communist party in Russia, primarily instigated by Stalin. He authorized the extermination of many Jewish leaders in the party as well as ordinary Jewish citizens. We cannot identify with certainty the reasons for this deep-rooted antagonism between Communist leaders and the Jews. It could be nationalism—that is, Russian Communists do not trust non-Russians. Consequently they might have used the Jews to foment revolution early in the century, then have them systematically removed from positions of power. But quite possibly the Communists felt intimidated by the intellectual gifts of their Jewish comrades.

Whatever the causes, one contributing factor was probably the indomitable will of the Jew. Communism is an ideology of force; no country would intelligently vote for a Communist government. The only free countries of the world that I can identify as having voted a Communist into office (1) were dominated by a Communist-controlled press, and (2) voted the Communists out of office at the next election. The Communists realize that they cannot intimidate the Jew. Because of the Jewish temperament—or possibly because of the many centuries of suffering—Jews cannot be bullied into silence. Consequently thousands of them have been placed in maximum security prisons and psychiatric hospitals throughout Siberia and other remote areas of the Soviet Union to keep them from stirring up trouble. Historically, only Adolf Hitler has been more inhumane than Russia in persecuting the Jews.

Not content just to silence Jewish opposition in Russia, the Communists are unwilling to permit the large Jewish population of the nation to emigrate. As I said earlier, almost 25 percent of the world's Jews live in Russia. According to reports coming to the West, most of them are discontented and eagerly desire an opportunity to migrate to Israel. But their efforts have been blocked at every turn.

It is made very clear in His Word that God would bless the nations that are good to the Jews and curse those that have persecuted them. In all history there has never been a case where a nation that has mistreated the Jews has conquered a nation that was benevolent to them. As we will see in a later chapter, America's policy of defending Israel is probably our greatest line of national defense. By contrast, Russia's policy of persecution will prove to be her death knell.

The day is coming when God will wreak judgment on Russia for her mistreatment of the Jews. Her doom is sealed, prescribed vividly in Ezekiel 38 and 39. That coming destruction is the subject of our next chapter.

7. The Coming Destruction of Russia

No rational person takes pleasure in the destruction of an entire nation, not even when that destruction is an act of judgment by a righteous, sovereign God. However, we must recognize that 2,500 years ago the Hebrew prophets, under inspiration of the Holy Spirit, made such a prediction, and world conditions seem to indicate that the coming destruction cannot be far off. Russia is unquestionably the nation identified in the prophecies of Ezekiel 38 and 39

It is not sufficient just to say that Bible scholars for several hundred years have interpreted Ezekiel 38 and 39 as referring to Russia. We must be more explicit than that, for the proper identity of "Gog" and "Magog" is essential to the interpretation of this passage. Therefore I suggest three reasons that confirm the identity of that nation, which is also predicted to invade Israel in the last days.

1. Russia's Philosophy

We have already seen in the Bible that God is against "Magog" (the country) and "Gog" (the chief prince of the country). Why would a loving God who has always been *for* mankind be against this nation? Because the nation is against *Him*. As the preceding chapter showed, "Magog" exhibits her antagonism toward God by opposing humanity, the special object of God's love; defying God's Word; and above all, antagonizing His people, the nation of Israel. Philosophically and religiously, the nation of Russia qualifies in every way. It is anti-God, anti-human, anti-Bible, and

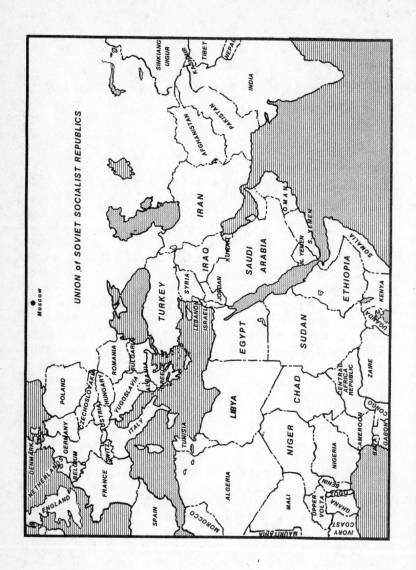

anti-Israel. But there is another reason for recognizing "Magog" as Russia.

2. Russia's Geographical Location

Another significant reason for identifying Russia as Magog is her geographical location. The Bible usually describes geography in relation to Israel. For example, "south" means south of Israel; "north" signifies north of Israel. The only likely exception would come in this instance, in that Ezekiel was in Babylon when he spoke the prophecy. A case could be made that he may have meant "north of Babylon" when he said, "You will come from your place in the far north" (38:15), or, "I will bring you from the far north and send you against the mountains of Israel" (39:2).

The map on the preceding page shows that it doesn't matter whether one starts in Israel or Babylon; north in either case leads to the broad expanse of the Soviet Union. Unquestionably the invading forces that will march against the nation Israel, recalled from the nations of the world and established in her own land, come from none other than Soviet Russia.

3. The Study of Etymology

Etymology is the study of linguistic changes and the history of words. We will investigate the etymology of the names of nations. As we shall see, "Magog" is an ancient name for the nation now known as Russia. "Gog" merely means "the chief prince of Magog," or more literally, the chief prince of "Meshech and Tubal" (38:2–3; 39:1).

Genesis 10 helps to establish the identity of these people. Magog was the second son of Japheth who, according to Josephus, the great Jewish historian, settled north of the Black Sea. Tubal and Meshech were the fifth and sixth sons of Japheth, and their descendants settled south of the Black Sea. It is believed that these people intermarried and became known as Magog, the dominant tribe. The name "Moscow" derives from the tribal name "Meshech," and "Tobolsk," the name of the principal state, from "Tubal." The noun "Gog" is from the original tribal name "Magog," which gradually became "Rash," then "Russ," and today is known as "Russia."

In *The Late Great Planet Earth,* Hal Lindsey offers a helpful discussion of the identity of these nations.

Dead Men Do Tell Tales!

It is necessary on the next few pages to establish some documentation from ancient history. Some people find this subject "a little dull," to say the least. If this is your case, you may wish to skim over the high points. For others, it will prove to be rewarding to check carefully the grounds upon which the historical case is built.

Herodotus, the fifth century B.C. Greek philosopher, is quoted as mentioning Meshech and Tubal. He identified them with a people named the Samaritans and Muschovites who lived at that time in the ancient province of Pontus in northern Asia Minor.

Josephus, a Jewish historian of the first century, says that the people of his day known as the Moschevi and Thobelites were founded by Meshech and Tubal, respectively. He said, ". . .Magog is called the Scythians by the Greeks." He continued by saying that these people lived in the northern regions above the Caucasus Mountains."

Pliny, a noted Roman writer of early Christian times, said, "Hierapolis, taken by the Scythians, was afterward called Magog." In this he shows that the dreaded barbaric people called the Scythians were identified with their ancient tribal name. Any good history book of ancient times traces the Scythians to be a principal part of the people who make up modern Russia.

Wilhelm Gesenius, a great Hebrew scholar of the early nineteenth century, discusses these words in his unsurpassed Hebrew Lexicon. "Meshech," he says, "was founder of the Moschi, a barbarous people, who dwelt in the Moschian mountains."

This scholar went on to say that the Greek name, "Moschi," derived from the Hebrew name Meshech is the source of the name for *the city of Moscow*. In discussing Tubal he said, "Tubal is the son of Rapheth, founder of the Tibereni, a people dwelling on the Black Sea to the west of the Moschi."

Gesenius concludes by saying that these people undoubtedly make up the modern Russian people.

There is one more name to consider in this line of evidence. It is the Hebrew word, "Rosh," translated "chief" in Ezekiel 38:2,3 of the King James and Revised Standard Versions. The word literally means in Hebrew the "top" or "head" of something. According to most scholars, this word is used in the sense of a proper name, not as a descriptive noun qualifying the word "prince."

The German scholar, Dr. Keil, says after a careful grammatical analysis that it should be translated as a proper name, i.e., Rosh. He says, "The Byzantine and Arabic writers frequently mention a people called Ros and Rus, dwelling in the country of Taurus, and reckoned among the Scythian tribes."

Dr. Gesenius in his Hebrew Lexicon says, ". . .Rosh was a designation for the tribes then north of the Taurus Mountains, dwelling in the neighborhood of the Volga."

He concluded that in this name and tribe we have the first historical trace of the Russ or Russian nation. [1]

In 1857 Rev. F. E. Pitts delivered two sermons on prophecy before a joint session of the houses of the U.S. Congress. His was one of the most respected prophetic voices of his day. Sixty years before the Communist conquest of Russia, he had the boldness to warn the United States government of the coming day when Russia would be a dominant world power. Obviously he had insight, unpopular in his day, derived from Ezekiel 38 and 39.

Pitts had access to prophetic literature that is no longer available—literature showing that more than a hundred years ago it was popular to identify "Rosh" as Russia.

The very name of the ancient patriarchs of the Russian dominions determine their location and nationality.

"Gog" signifies a prince or head of many countries.

"Magog, Gomer, Meshech, and Tubal" are four of the seven sons of Japheth (see Genesis 10, I Chronicles 1).

These patriarchs, according to Calmet, Brown, Bochart, and others, settled within the bounds of what is now the Russian dominions.

"Magog," says Josephus, "founded the Magogue, whom the Greeks call Sythee," the Scyth who form almost one-fourth of Russian population. They extended from Hungary, Transylvania, and Wallachia, on the west, to the River Dan on the east. The Russian territory of this people embraces a large portion both of Europe and Asia.

"Meshech," the sixth son of Japheth, settled in the northeastern portion of Asia Minor. His posterity extended from the shores of the Euxine [Black] Sea along to the south of the Caucasus. He was the father of the Rossi and Moschi, who dispersed their colonies over a vast portion of Russian territory. And their names are preserved in

[1]Hal Lindsey with C. C. Carlson, *The Late Great Planet Earth* (Grand Rapids: Zondervan, 1970, 1977), 52-54. Used by permission.

the names of Russians and Moscovites to this day. The Septuagint version of the Old Testament renders the term "Meshech" by the words "Mosch" and "Rosch"; while "Moscovy' is a common name for Russia, and the city of Moscow is one of her principal cities.

"Tubal," or Tobal, the fifth son of Japheth, settled beyond the Caspian and Black seas in the eastern possessions of Russia, embracing a very large portion of these dominions. The name of this patriarch is still preserved in the river Tobal, which waters an immense tract of Russian territory; and the city of Tobalski in Russia is still a monument to this son of Japheth.

From all which, it is certain that, as Magog, Meshech, and Tubal compose the present possessions of Russia, the sovereignty of that empire is the chief prince addressed in the prophetic message.

We must look to Russia, then, as the colossal giant of reconstructed monarchy, embodying the show of autocracy in the last grand organization—embracing all the principles foreshadowed in the metallic symbol of the vision "whose brightness was excellent, and the form thereof terrible." In fact, the Emperor of all the Russians still bears the royal cognomen of the golden-headed monarchs of ancient Babylon. Who is the present Emperor of Russia? Alexander the Czar. And who are found among the monarchs of Assyria? Nobonazar, Nebuchadnezzar, and Belshazzar. These were not accidental terminations of their respective names, but were doubtless terms of Assyrian royalty. So also the Roman Caesars, which scarcely vary from the true pronunciation of the czars. We behold in Russia the original trunk of autocracy. In the time of Catharine, she arose in august magnitude, and entered into the European state system about the time of the rise of our great country. We see rising on the one hand and on the other, the two great powers that represent respectively their opposing principles of government that will come in collision in the last dreadful fray. [2]

In the light of the evidence that is available, we are not surprised that students of prophecy foresaw Russia's role as a world power years ago—long before her country showed any signs of greatness. Bishop Lowth of England wrote in 1710, "Rosh, taken as a proper name, in Ezekiel signifies the inhabitants of Scythia, from whom the modern Russians derive their name." [3]

It should be remembered that most of these quotations were written many years before the Bolshevik Revolution and the rise of Russia to power. Bible scholars anticipated Russia becoming a dominant power in the end time while she was literally a

---

[2]F. E. Pitts, *The U.S.A. in Prophecy* (Baltimore: J. W. Bull, 1862).

[3]John Cumming, *The Destiny of Nations* (London: Hurst & Blackette, 1864).

nonentity as a nation. Early in this century she was still a second-rate influence in the affairs of nations; in 1905 little Japan defeated Russia in the Russo-Japanese War.

Why Will Russia Attack Israel?

During the past sixty years Russian diplomats and foreign policy strategists have proved that they are much smarter than their Western counterparts. Every time our diplomats engage them in conference, we lose land, friends, people, or rights. What would make a superpower like Russia at the end time abandon the path of diplomacy and attack the little nation of Israel? There are four possible reasons.

1. Russia's longstanding hatred of the Jews

It is clear from history that the Jews cannot be intimidated by the Russians or anyone else. We can be certain that the Russians are not pleased with Israel's four military victories since 1949. It is highly possible that the Russians will finally decide that they cannot defeat the Israelis through their Arab allies without personally engaging them on the field of combat. This decision could be the one that summons them to march against Israel.

2. Plunder, spoil, and wealth

In Ezekiel 38:12–13 we read,

> "I will plunder and loot and turn my hand against the resettled ruins and the people gathered from the nations, rich in livestock and goods, living at the center of the land." Sheba and Dedan and the merchants of Tarshish and all her villages will say to you, "Have you come to plunder? Have you gathered your hordes to loot, to carry off silver and gold, to take away livestock and goods and to seize much plunder?"

These verses seem to suggest two important possibilities. One is that the economic conditions of Israel are destined to improve and those of the Soviet Union deteriorate. We have already seen that as a result of the peace treaties made between the Jews and the Arabs, Israel will experience a time of phenomenal material blessing, making her an object of greed on the part of the Russian dictators.

The future is not so bright for Russia. One way in which God has manifested his displeasure with Russia as a nation during the past six decades lies in her total economic failure under communism. The Crimea was known under the czars as "the breadbasket of the world." The wheat harvested there was bountiful and more than sufficient for the needs of the Russian people; large quantities were exported to other nations of Europe.

Since the Russian Revolution, however, the severe weather of the Soviet Union has worsened, producing some of the harshest winters on record. Russia has become notorious for poor wheat crops—partly because of the weather and partly because of the lack of motivation among the Russian people under communism. Reports from Russia that scientists have desperately tried to manipulate the weather are probably fraudulent; if they are true, they give evidence that the scientific endeavors have not worked or have even made the situation worse. Economic judgment from God is destined to continue, bringing the need to purchase increasing quantities of foreign grain.

3. God's sovereign will

The primary reason why Russia will invade Israel is that God has decreed it. Ezekiel 38:3–4, 8 declares,

> This is what the Sovereign LORD says: . . . "I will turn you around, put hooks in your jaws and bring you out with your whole army— your horses, your horsemen fully armed, and a great horde with large and small shields, all of them brandishing their swords. . . .After many days you will be called to arms. In future years you will invade a land that has recovered from war, whose people were gathered from many nations to the mountains of Israel, which had long been desolate. They had been brought out from the nations, and now all of them live in safety."

Ezekiel 39:2 adds, "I will turn you around and drag you along. I will bring you from the far north and send you against the mountains of Israel."

"This is what the Sovereign LORD says: On that day thoughts will come into your mind and you will devise an evil scheme" (Ezekiel 38:10).

The attack on Israel is conceived and mobilized by almighty God. This implies that God will stir the Russians' greedy plan, fulfilling Ezekiel 38:4: "I will put hooks in your jaws and bring you out."

In studying these two chapters of Ezekiel, I sense that God will pour out His wrath upon Russia not only to demonstrate His power, but also to heap judgment on those who have persecuted human beings, especially Israel.

The prophetic scenario is plain: Russia does not have Israel as her *primary* target. Russia's major objective has admittedly been world conquest. One way in which the Communists have been consistent for the last seventy years is in their implacable movement toward that primary objective. God has proclaimed that He raises up whom He will and puts down whom He will (Ezekiel 21:26; Daniel 4:34–35). Even at the end time, when Russia reigns as a superpower, God will still be in control, for He is able to "put hooks in her jaw" and lead her to obey His will.

4. A matter of safety

We have said that Israel is the third most powerful nation in the world, particularly if we limit that assessment to nations within a thousand miles of her homeland. Apart from world conquest, what is the chief objective of the Soviet Union? To conquer the United States of America. If America were to fall into the hands of the Soviets, they could quickly seize control of the rest of the world.

At present no one really knows whether the United States' military forces are more powerful than Russia's or whether our government leaders will have the moral courage and national will to oppose Russia when these climactic events occur. Many knowledgeable people believe that the mood in this country is so antiwar as to be anti-self-defense, that many would prefer to capitulate to Communist domination rather than to fight.

My point, however, is that no one—not even the Russians—really knows whether they would be victorious in a first-strike attack against the United States. Therefore, before attacking the United States, they would surely attempt to nullify military assistance from any other source on earth. The government of Israel is pragmatic enough to know that if Russia attacks the United States, Israel herself would be the next target. Therefore the Soviet military leadership may theorize that an invasion of Israel must precede a frontal assault on the leader of the Western world. Consequently an invasion of Israel may be just one more step in the fulfillment of their objective of world conquest.

Russia's Allies in the Attack on Israel

The only war that Russia has ever fought alone is being lost—against Afghanistan. We can be certain that the Russians will not invade Israel alone. The prophet stipulates that they will bring "many nations with you, . . .hordes gathered about you" (Ezekiel 38:6–7). But he also notes that Russia will be in command (v. 7).

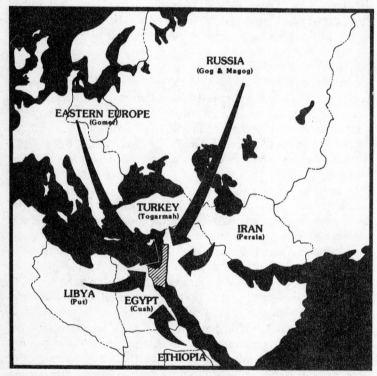

Russia's confederates, as disclosed in Ezekiel 38:5–6, are among her current friends. Those not in her orbit of friends at present are being cultivated either secretly or openly. Hal

Lindsey offers interesting suggestions as to the identity of Russia's allies.

> All authorities agree on who Persia is today. It is modern Iran. This is significant because it is being wooed to join the United Arab Republic in its hostility against Israel. The Russians are at this moment seeking to gain footholds in Iran by various overtures of aid.[4]

Secret information coming out of Iran indicates that the Ayatollah is not at all well, and careful plans have been laid that on the event of his death a ruler favorable to Russia will be established as a leader. It would not be surprising if Russia invaded Iran, if it seemed necessary to achieve her ends, particularly now that Iran is weakened militarily and economically through her war with Iraq.

Lindsey continues,

> In order to mount the large-scale invasion predicted by Ezekiel, Russia would need Iran as an ally. It would be much more difficult to move a large land army across the Caucasus Mountains that border Turkey, than the Elburz Mountains that border Iran. Iran's general terrain is also much easier to cross than Turkey's. Transportation, however, will be needed through both countries.

Ethiopia or Cush (Black African Nations)

Ethiopia is a translation of the Hebrew word, *Cush*. Cush was the first son of Ham, one of the sons of Noah.

Moses mentions "the land of Cush" as originally being adjacent to an area near the Tigris and Euphrates rivers (Genesis 2:13).

After examining many authorities on the subject, the writer discovered once again why Dr. Gesenius is recognized as one of the great scholars of history. Gesenius summarized all of the evidence as follows: (1) The Cushites were black men. (2) They migrated first to the Arabian peninsula and then across the Red Sea to the area south of Egypt. (3) All the black people of Africa are descended from Cush. . . .

Cush is translated "Ethiopia" twenty-one times in the King James Version, which is somewhat misleading. It is certain that the ancient Ethiopians (modern Abyssinia) are made up of Cushites, but they do not represent all of them, according to history.

The sobering conclusion is this: many of the African nations will be united and allied with the Russians in the invasion of Israel. This is in

---

[4]Lindsey with Carlson, *The Late Great Planet Earth*, 56.

accord with Daniel's graphic description of this invasion (Daniel 11:36–45).

The Russian force is called "the King of the North" and the sphere of power which the African (Cush) will be a part of is called "the King of the South."

One of the most active areas for the Communist "gospel" is in Africa. As we see further developments in this area in the future, we realize that it will become converted to Communism.

Libya or Put (Arabic African Nations)

Libya is the translation of the original Hebrew word, *Put*. We have the same problem pinpointing these people as with Cush. Put was the third son of Ham (Genesis 10:6). The descendants of Put migrated to the land west of Egypt and became the source of the North African Arab nations, such as Libya, Algeria, Tunisia, and Morocco. The first settlement of Put was called Libya by the ancient historian, Josephus, and Pliny. The Greek translation of the Hebrew Old Testament, called the Septuagint, translates Put as Libya in about 165 B.C.

The conclusion is that Russia's ally, Put, certainly included more than what is now called Libya. Once again there are current events to show the beginning of this alliance.

The territory of Northern Africa is becoming solidly pro-Soviet. Algeria appears to be already Communist and allied with Russia.

As we watch this area in the next few years we shall see indications that it is destined to join the southern sphere of power which will attack Israel along with the "King of the North."

Gomer and All Its Hordes (Iron Curtain Countries)

Gomer was the eldest son of Japheth, and the father of Ashkenaz, Riphath, and Togarmah. These people make up an extremely important part of the future Russian invasion force.

Dr. Young, citing the best of the most recent archaeological finds, says of Gomer and his hordes, "They settled on the north of the Black Sea, and then spread themselves southward and westward to the extremities of Europe."

Gesenius speaks of part of Gomer's "hordes" as being Ashkenaz. . . . "the proper name of a region and a nation in northern Asia, sprung from the Cimmerians who are the ancient people of Gomer. The modern Jews understand it to be Germany, and call that country by this Hebrew name. . . ."

Josephus called the sons of Ashkenaz, "The Rheginians," and a map of the ancient Roman Empire places them in the area of modern Poland, Czechoslovakia, and East Germany to the banks of the Danube River. The modern Jewish Talmud confirms the same geographical picture.

The conclusion is that Gomer and its hordes are a part of the vast area of modern Eastern Europe which is totally behind the Iron Curtain. This includes East Germany and the Slovak countries.

Togarmah and All Its Hordes
(Southern Russia and the Cossacks)

In Ezekiel 38:6 "the house of Togarmah, and all its hordes" are specifically pointed out as being from "the uttermost north.". . .

Dr. Bauman traces evidence of some of the sons of Togarmah to the Turkoman tribes in central Asia. This would explain the statement, ". . .of the uttermost north, and all its hordes."

The conclusion is that Togarmah is part of modern Southern Russia and is probably the origin of the Cossacks and other people of the Eastern part of Russia. It is interesting to note that the Cossacks have always loved horses and have been recognized as producing the finest army of cavalry in the world. Today they are reported to have several divisions of cavalry. It is believed by some military men that cavalry will actually be used in the invasion of the Middle East just as Ezekiel and other prophets literally predicted. During the Korean War the Red Chinese proved that in rugged mountainous terrain, horses are still the fastest means of moving a large attacking force into battle zones.

Isn't it a coincidence that such terrain stands between Russia and the Israeli?

Many People Are With You

Ezekiel indicates that he hasn't given a complete list of allies. Enough is given, however, to make this writer amazed by the number of people and nations which will be involved.

Gog, Take Command

Ezekiel, prophetically addressing the Russian ruler, commands him to ". . .be prepared; yes, prepare yourself, you and all your companies that are assembled about you, and you be a guard *and* commander for them" (Ezekiel 38:7 Amplified).

In other words, the Russian ruler is to equip his confederates with arms and to assume command.

If you have doubts about all that has been said in this chapter, isn't it a bit unnerving to note that almost all of the countries predicted as part of this great army are already armed with weapons created and manufactured in Russia [or her satellite nations]?

What's Your Name, Gog?

We have seen that Russia will arm and equip a vast confederacy. This powerful group of allies will lead an attack on restored Israel. However, Russia and her confederates will be destroyed completely by an act that Israel will acknowledge as being from their God. This

act will bring many in Israel to believe in their true Messiah (Ezekiel
38:15ff.) [5]

Additional insight is found in the address delivered by the Rev.
F. E. Pitts before the U. S. Congress more than 135 years ago.

"Gomer, and all his bands; the house of Togarmah of the north
quarters, and all his bands, and many people with thee" [Ezekiel
38:6].

"Gomer," another son of Japheth, settled farther down westward
in Europe; and has left his name entailed in Hungary, in a city and
country both known to this day as the city and country of Gomer.

"Togarmah," the son of Gomer, according to Cicero and Strabo,
not only peopled a large portion of Western Europe, but sent
settlements into Turcomania and Scythia in Russia.

Russia, then, according to the Scriptures, is the headship or leading
power around which the multitudinous armies of allied monarchy
shall be gathered together.

"Persia, Ethiopia, and Libya with them; all of them with shield and
helmet" [Ezekiel 38:5].

Persia here represents the swarming hosts from the Asiatic
possessions; Ethiopia, Libya, and the armies of Africa.

"Thou shalt ascend and come like a storm, thou shalt be like a
cloud to cover the land, thou, and all thy bands, and many people
with thee" [Ezekiel 38:9].

The invasion is here announced by an armament such as the world
never saw. For the millions that are to assemble under Gog or Russia
embrace nearly all of Europe, as well as a large portion of Asia and
Africa. This army is drafted from three continents to invade a fourth.
It rises dismal as a cloud, and dreadful as a storm. [6]

From all this we learn that a dominant leader, called Gog,
described as the "chief prince of Rosh," is going to arise and
lead Russia into a vast northeastern confederation of nations
including Iran, Ethiopia and other African nations, Germany,
Armenia, possibly Turkey, conceivably some orientals, and
whoever else can be included with the statement, 'And many
peoples with thee." This group of nations, headed by Russia,
will advance against Israel in the last days.

On the strength of this passage from the Book of Ezekiel I
predicted in my book *The Beginning of the End* that the "troika"

[5]Ibid., 56-60. Used by permission.
[6]Pitts, *The U.S.A. in Prophecy.*

leadership that was then the policy in the Soviet Union would soon pass away.[7] I stated that Russian preparedness for the coming invasion of Israel would feature one strong, dominant leader. The accuracy of that prediction appears in the fact that the "troika"—leadership shared by three persons—is no longer fashionable in Moscow.

The Russian Invasion of Israel

Some 2,500 years ago the Hebrew prophet Ezekiel described in considerable detail the circumstances under which Communist Russia and her hordes of anti-Semitic nations would attempt to invade the little nation of Israel.

> "I will turn you around, put hooks in your jaws and bring you out with your whole army—your horses, your horsemen fully armed, and a great horde with large and small shields, all of them brandishing their swords. . . .
>
> "After many days you will be called to arms. In future years you will invade a land that has recovered from war, whose people were gathered from many nations to the mountains of Israel, which had long been desolate. They had been brought out from the nations, and now all of them live in safety. You and all your troops and the many nations with you will go up, advancing like a storm; you will be like a cloud covering the land. . . .
>
> "You will come from your place in the far north, you and many nations with you, all of them riding on horses, a great horde, a mighty army. You will advance against my people Israel like a cloud that covers the land. In days to come, O Gog, I will bring you against my land, so that the nations may know me when I show myself holy through you before their eyes" (Ezekiel 38:4, 8–9, 15–16).

There are two legitimate ways to interpret the kind of weapons used in this prophecy—literally and symbolically. Bible-believing scholars can be found on either side.

A literal interpretation of the passage suggests that modern methods of warfare will someday become obsolete and man will return to primitive weapons. That is not as far-fetched as it may appear at first. For years electronic scientists have reportedly been working on heat-ray devices that would have the capacity

[7]Tim LaHaye, *The Beginning of the End* (Wheaton, Ill.: Tyndale House Publishers, 1979).

to render metallic surfaces so hot they could not be touched for many miles. If such an invention were produced by the West, Russia could not invade Israel with tanks, bazookas, and modern weaponry. They would have to resort to horses. Metal weapons would be replaced with wooden; these would not be wooden swords and spears as used in ancient days, but implements fashioned with enormous strength out of basic wood materials, seasoned with resin, or lignostone, or other chemically treated woods that already are used industrially and have an amazingly long burn life.

If, on the other hand, the passage is to be taken symbolically, the prophet Ezekiel is merely describing implements of war in terms meaningful to his contemporary audience. We must always remember that the Bible was written to specific people at a specific time and must therefore be meaningful to them. If the prophet 2,500 years ago had addressed himself to tanks, half-tracks, aircraft carriers, and airplanes, no one would have understood what he meant.

Regardless which approach we take in interpreting this passage of Scripture, Russia will mount a massive military attack on Israel, and only God will be Israel's defense. God's supernatural intervention will save her.

"The hordes" who join Russia in this invasion

Russia almost never does anything alone. We have already seen that when they pursue a goal unilaterally, as in Afghanistan, they get bogged down in an endless war. That is usually not Russia's style. Instead, she prefers to supply the military technology and money to her satraps, such as the Palestine Liberation Organization, Cuba, Syria, or Egypt. Consequently, when Russia comes down to invade Israel, she will use Middle East hatred of the Jews to her advantage and inveigle these nations to help her in the fighting.

This will probably be the most massive invasion army assembled in the history of the world—all in opposition to Israel, a nation of less than 4 million people. For the first time since World War II, Israel's friends will betray her.

Two confederations of nations

I am convinced, for two reasons, that the invasion described by Ezekiel is not the Battle of Armageddon—warfare between Jesus Christ and the nations—described in Revelation 16. First, at this time there will be two leagues of nations: the northeastern confederation that invades with Russia, and the western confederation that has befriended Israel in the past. Second, in Ezekiel's account only a certain number from the armies of the world will march against the Jews. In the Battle of Armageddon, armies will come from all the countries of the world against Christ—not Israel. Yet, while this warfare will not be the real Battle of Armageddon, to the participants it will seem like it.

The northeastern confederation

We have already identified some of the nations that will join Russia. Actually six countries will constitute the northeastern confederation:
1. Russia, the instigator and leader;
2. Persia (Iran). If the Soviets can somehow repair the breach between Iraq and Iran, the former may also be included;
3. Ethiopia (Cush), which could involve Libya and representatives from many other African nations.
4. Gomer (Germany) "and its hordes," involving either just East Germany and the Soviet satellite countries of Eastern Europe, or all of Germany and the Eastern European satellites.
5. Togarmah "and its hordes"—Armenia, which may well involve Turkey and other nations or peoples remaining from the Turkish Empire.

Who needs a diplomatic note?

The western confederation of nations also appears in Ezekiel's prophecy.

> "Sheba and Dedan and the merchants of Tarshish and all her villages will say to you, 'Have you come to plunder? Have you gathered your hordes to loot, to carry off silver and gold, to take away livestock and goods and to seize much plunder?'" (Ezekiel 38:13).

Who are these nations that greet force with diplomacy? There is little doubt that the western confederation comprises the democracies of the West, principally the United States, Great Britain, and Canada. "Sheba and Dedan and the merchants of Tarshish" were the seafaring Phoenicians, many of whom migrated to Europe, particularly the British Isles and Spain. These countries, the colonizers of the seventeenth and eighteenth centuries, provide the only vigorous anti-Communist spirit in the world today.

The American Standard version renders "Tarshish and her villages" in verse 13 as "Tarshish and her young lions [or strong lions]." For this reason, many Bible scholars identify America, Canada, Australia, and other western democracies as the "cubs" of Great Britain and Spain, the colonizers of the West. Certainly that is historically valid. Therefore this probably does identify the nations of the prophecy. If the invasion were to take place in the decades of the eighties or the nineties, the western democracies would qualify.

It stands to reason that Russia does not take the entire world with her against Israel. At a time when two confederations of nations exist—basically Communist vs. anti-Communist—Israel is allied with the anti-Communists, as it is today.

Unfortunately for Israel, instead of meeting Communist force with force, the western democracies will meet the invasion with diplomacy. This historically represents the weak response of the democracies in both the world wars and in almost every conflict since. Instead of sending help at the moment when Israel needs the support of her allies, they will send a diplomatic note (perhaps through the United Nations) that essentially inquires of Russia and her hordes, "What are you going to do in little Israel—loot and carry away silver and gold, take away livestock and goods, and seize many riches?"

This may be the most breathtaking, dramatic moment in the history of modern Israel. Until this time, Israel could depend at least on the United States of America.

I well recall an incident that occurred as I jogged along a Mediterranean beach during one of my trips to Israel. A young English-speaking college student—an Israeli—began to jog with me, and we started a conversation when he discovered that I was an American. As we discussed Israel's victory in the Six-Day war, I asked if it ever occurred to him that Russia might someday invade Israel herself instead of sending the Arab nations. Pointing through the evening fog that was settling on the waters of the Mediterranean Sea (where the U.S. Seventh Fleet sailed in military splendor), he responded, "Oh, we're not worried about that; we know America would come to our rescue!"

I reflected with sorrow upon Ezekiel's prophecy that Israel's friends would *not* always come to her aid. When Russia's invasion forces rattle their spears, the western democracies, including America, will use the impotent instrument of diplomacy instead of the one power that all terrorists, murderers, dictators, and lawless individuals or nations understand: force. In the history of the world, no nation except Switzerland has ever enjoyed peace through weakness, and her peace was only an accommodation by the militaristic nations of the world wars to maintain free access to the exchange of money. All other nations have found that peace comes exclusively through strength.

The use of diplomacy at this strategic time in prophetic history would indicate that the western democracies will continue to dissipate their strength and military might while Russia builds her power base, nuclear or otherwise.

Nevertheless, when she finds herself confronted by her enemies and betrayed by her allies, the little nation of Israel, who has not set her heart toward God since returning to the Promised Land, will turn to Him in desperation—and in that moment find Him a ready deliverer.

God Delivers Israel

The scenario that develops at this point in our prophetic story is exciting. Confronted by overwhelming forces from Russia and forsaken by her friends, Israel will turn to God, and He will do for modern Israel what He did for ancient Israel. As the God over all forces, He will deliver Israel from the hands of the oppressor. As certain as it is that Russia and her Middle East hordes will come down against Israel, so certain is it that God will destroy the invading forces and deliver Israel supernaturally.

The prophet does not leave us in doubt as to the methods that God will use in this destruction. It is noteworthy that this is not the first time they will have been used by the Almighty, for all of them have precedence in the Old Testament.

1. A mighty earthquake

"In my zeal and fiery wrath I declare that at that time there shall be a great earthquake in the land of Israel. The fish of the sea, the birds of the air, the beasts of the field, every creature that moves along the ground, and all the people on the face of the earth will tremble at my presence. The mountains will be overturned, the cliffs will crumble and every wall will fall to the ground" (Ezekiel 38:19–20).

Evidently God permits the Russians and their hordes to begin an airborne invasion while the infantry launches a ground assault. But at a strategic moment He generates a powerful and destructive earthquake that causes people to "tremble" at His presence. This catastrophe will manifest the power of a supernatural God. Earthquakes were, of course, used by God in ancient days; Amos 1:1 and Zechariah 14:5 recount the terrible earthquake that rocked the land of Palestine in the days of Uzziah, king of Judah. It was no doubt a special intervention of God that caused that earthquake.

Jesus predicted that earthquakes would be one of the signs of His return and the end of the age (Matthew 24:7–8). The record shows that we have experienced an alarming increase in earthquakes during the past fifty years. One seismologist has stated that in each of the past five decades, the number and severity of earthquakes have surpassed the preceding decade.

We should also remember that the Book of Revelation predicts that during the first quarter of the Tribulation, a mighty earthquake will create havoc throughout the entire world (6:12–17). Another earthquake in the middle of the Tribulation will rock the city of Jerusalem (Revelation 11:13), and still another at the end of the Tribulation could well be the mightiest earthquake ever to shake the earth (Revelation 16:17–21). Consequently it is not unlike God to use His power to create earthquakes in defense of Israel when Russia's armies come against her.

2. The sword of the Lord

"I will summon a sword against Gog on all my mountains, declares the Sovereign LORD. Every man's sword will be against his brother" (Ezekiel 38:21).

Nothing shakes man from his independence and false sense of security like an earthquake, particularly one having the magnitude that God will provide for Israel's deliverance. And because

Israel is no match for the invading hordes of military personnel about to devour her, the Lord will confuse her enemies, and they will do battle with each other. If they are using tanks, they will train them on each other. If they are using airplanes, they will dogfight against their own planes. Or if, as already indicated, they have reverted to more primitive weapons of warfare, Israel's enemies will skirmish among themselves rather than against their originally intended foe.

One precedent for such an incredible event appears in Judges 7:8-22, where the story is told of a large army becoming so confused that the the soldiers attacked each other and fled in fright from a mere three hundred Israelites.

3. Plague and bloodshed

"I will execute judgment upon him with plague and bloodshed. . ." (Ezekiel 38:22).

History shows that plagues have often accompanied the wanton killing of human beings in battle. Human carnage, blood, and the remains of a battlefield breed disease. But in the case of Russia's invasion of Israel, the plague seems to be something uniquely manipulated by God to further destroy the effectiveness of the enemy. The next judgment to befall the invaders is a plaguelike pestilence that causes much bloodshed. Pestilence associated with the aftermath of war is similar to that foretold by our Lord in Matthew 24. Those who survive the earthquake and the hand-to-hand combat will certainly perish in the plague.

4. Floods

". . .I will pour down torrents of rain, hailstones and burning sulfur on him and on his troops and on the many nations with him" (Ezekiel 38:22).

The portion of the invading force that is left after the earthquake, the fighting, and the plague will be destroyed by hailstones and burning sulfur.

For those who interpret this verse literally, there are Old Testament precedents both in the destruction God reigned down on Sodom and Gomorrah and in some of the battles of Israel. For example, Joshua 10:11 states that when Joshua's armies fought against the Amorites, "The LORD hurled large hailstones down on them from the sky, and more of them died from the hailstones than were killed by the swords of the Israelites.''

This final stage in God's judgment on the invaders could create not only a muddy terrain that would bog down any military advance, but also flooding conditions that would imperil human life.

5. Burning sulfur

The use of burning sulfur as a means of judgment recalls the destruction of Sodom and Gomorrah, with both earthquake and fire and brimstone—that is, burning sulfur. The troops who survive the other four judgments will die as a result of the falling burning sulfur. No wonder God says in Ezekiel 39:4, "On the mountains of Israel you will fall, you and all your troops and the nations with you.''

These five judgments of God will result in the annihilation of the armies of Gog and her allies. This will undoubtedly be the greatest holocaust fulfilled in a single day in the history of the world. But there is more.

God Destroys the Spies "in the Isles"

"Persia, Cush and Put will be with them, all with shields and helmets, also Gomer with all its troops, and Beth Togarmah from the far north with all its troops—the many nations with you" (Ezekiel 38:5–6).

As a special demonstration to the world of God's omnipotence, Ezekiel gives an unusual prophecy. God will not only destroy the entire army of Magog, but also consume with fire those who "live in safety in the coastlands.'' The word "coastlands'' is understood by Bible scholars to mean "the nations''; some older translations render it "in the isles.''

Who would qualify as those who live in nations not involved in the conflict? They could be individuals who live in safety or security on islands, or this could refer to uninvolved coastland nations. The verse probably refers to the many Communist spies and sympathizers who live in the western democracies—who regularly take advantage of their freedom by pursuing subversion for the cause of Moscow and the Kremlin. Such spies or

Communist infiltrators occupy many key positions throughout America—in the bureaucracy, universities and colleges, and the media—and subvert the minds of our citizens.

These people who have spent much of their adult life betraying the country that gives them freedom and safety will suddenly be consumed by fire. The United States will not have to reactivate the House Un-American Activities Committee to administer justice. Rather, the God who knows "the thoughts and intents of the heart" will judge these traitors by fire. We can only imagine the number of vacancies that will occur in one day in the federal and state governments and in the three thousand universities and colleges of America. In all likelihood this same judgment will create similar vacancies in Canada, Australia, and the British Isles. At the United Nations, divine fire judgment will suddenly fall and reveal the identity of those who really are Communist spies or sympathizers. Such an event will create electrifying headlines.

The World in Chaos—Time for the Antichrist

Can you imagine the chaos into which the world's nations will be plunged the day after God destroys not only the invading armies of Russia, but also the Communist spies in the Western world? On the one hand, the skeptical attitude of the secular humanists toward the existence of God will suddenly be confronted with irrefutable evidence of a supernatural God. There will be absolutely no other explanation for these events. In addition, many trusted leaders in key positions of influence will have been destroyed by fire because they were traitors to their country.

Probably the greatest result of this chaos is that western democratic leaders who survive will become the dominant leaders of the world. The threat of worldwide Communism will have been destroyed in a single day, leaving Israel and the western confederation of nations in a world-dominating position.

We cannot be certain what will occur politically immediately after this awesome event. But I believe that the rising tide of interest in world government under the guise of "the new world order" will suddenly find little opposition. With Communism removed as a world threat, the humanistic politicians of the world may naturally assume that a one-world government—within either the United Nations or its replacement—should provide the solution to this planet's ills. All this will prepare the way for the Antichrist to consolidate the nations in preparation for the day when he signs a covenant with Israel and ushers in the great tribulation period spoken of so frequently by our Lord and the Hebrew prophets.

Of this we can be certain: all the world will momentarily stand in awe of the supernatural God in heaven who, after 1,900 years of silence, has spoken in terms that even the most unbelieving can understand. We will write of this in a later chapter.

8. When Will Russia Be Destroyed?

The event described in the last chapter—the destruction of Russia—could be the most momentous episode in the last 1,900 years of human history. It will probably occur in your lifetime.

"When Shall These Things Be?"

Whenever we discuss the future events of Bible prophecy, someone immediately asks, "When will this take place?" Admittedly, Bible teachers do not concur as to the "when" of this event. But for at least four reasons it cannot be fused with the Battle of Armageddon.

1. Armageddon is not directed against Israel, but constitutes an attack on the part of the world's nations against Christ (see Revelation 16:12–21 and 19:11–21).The deception of the Antichrist and his insane hatred of Jesus Christ at the end of the tribulation period will culminate with his bringing together—even from the Orient over the dried-up river Euphrates—hordes of people against, not Israel, but Jesus Christ, the coming King. That he will utterly fail is clearly predicted in Revelation 19. However, this Scripture passage should not be confused with Ezekiel 38 and 39, which to even a casual reader plainly states that Israel is the object of Gog and Magog's hatred. These two attacks are unique and distinct, and I believe they will occur at least ten or more years apart.

2. No one-world government is functioning during the events in Ezekiel 38 and 39. The destruction of Russia, as revealed by God to His prophet, will come at a time when—as we have

already seen—Israel is the central focus of two confederations of nations. These two confederations—the northeastern confederation of Russia and her hordes vs. the western democracies that do not come to the aid of Israel, cannot coexist in the one-world government predicted by our Lord and His prophets for the seven-year Tribulation.

3. Gog comes from the North, the Antichrist from Europe. Gog the prince and Magog the country are predicted to come from the "north parts" (Ezekiel 38:15). According to Daniel 7:8, 24, and 26, the Antichrist comes out of Rome, a mixed blood of Romans, Greeks, and possibly Jews. [1]

4. It takes seven years to burn the implements of war (Ezekiel 39:8–10). Armageddon occurs at the end of the Tribulation just before the Millennium. This in turn, according to 2 Peter 3, begins with a renovation of the earth by fire. It is certain that the Jews will not spend the first seven winters of the Millennium burning the implements of war left over from the Tribulation.

Taking these four reasons together, we can only conclude that Ezekiel 38 and 39 are not to be confused with Armageddon. Instead, they occur ten or more years earlier, prior to the tribulation period.

When Does Israel Burn War Implements?

In Ezekiel 39:8–10 we find that after Russia has been supernaturally destroyed, "those who live in the towns of Israel will go out and use the weapons for fuel and burn them up. . . .For seven years they will use them for fuel." Obviously the Israelis are not going to pile all the war implements together and make an enormous bonfire. In a land that enjoys quite mild winters, they will use the weapons for fuel for seven seasons instead of gathering firewood from the forests.

Two facts stand out in bold relief. First, Israel will enjoy seven years of peace *after* Russia is destroyed; second, for seven winters they will be reminded of God's supernatural intervention on their behalf as they burn the implements of war. It is vitally important that we locate these seven years chronologically,

---

[1]Tim LaHaye, *Revelation—Illustrated and Made Plain* (Grand Rapids: Zondervan, 1975).

because they are the key to the period in which the Soviet Union will be destroyed.

God has not left us without information regarding His plans for the future. The first chart in this chapter reflects the major basic events accepted by almost all scholars who hold a pretribulationist view of prophecy. The chart specifies that the Antichrist breaks his covenant with Israel during the latter 3 1/2 years of the Tribulation. According to Revelation 12, this event will unleash the harshest anti-Semitic persecution the world has ever known—a fiery furnace arranged for the Jews by the Antichrist. Russia will have to be destroyed *at least* 3 1/2 years *before* the Tribulation begins, for the Jews to have seven years in which to burn the implements of war.

On the second chart, this detail has been added with the thought in mind that there is no reason necessitating the Jews' burning the weapons during the first 3 1/2 years of the Tribulation. The entire seven-year period of burning could occur *before* the Tribulation begins, but there is no way to be certain of this. We can only speculate as to whether the seven-year period occurs entirely before the Tribulation. We know that it cannot extend beyond the Tribulation.

What About the Rapture?

Most premillennial scholars place the rapture of the church before the Tribulation.[2] The biggest misconception of some pretribulationists is that the second coming of Christ for His church (the Rapture) and the beginning of the tribulation period are simultaneous. They may be, but no passage of Scripture requires it. We must remember that the Tribulation is not started by the rapture of the church but by the signing of the covenant between the Antichrist and Israel.

Admittedly, 1 Thessalonians 4:17–18 and 2 Thessalonians 2—which describe the Rapture, the Tribulation, and the revelation of the man of sin or Antichrist—parallel the signing of the covenant. But it is important not to tie them together. The

²See Tim LaHaye, *The Beginning of the End* (Wheaton, Ill.: Tyndale House Publishers, 1979), chs. 1 and 2; and Tim LaHaye, *Revelation—Illustrated and Made Plain* (Grand Rapids: Zondervan, 1975), 75-76.

The most-accepted understanding of pretribulationist prophecy.

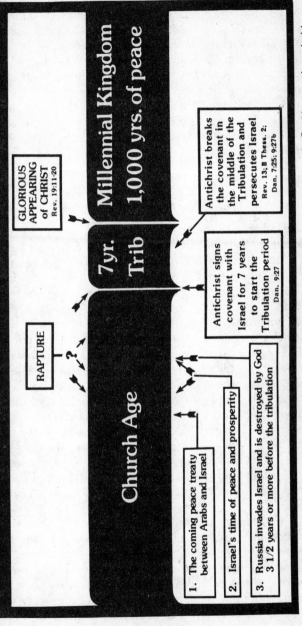

THE NEXT MAJOR PROPHETIC EVENTS

RAPTURE	GLORIOUS APPEARING of CHRIST Rev. 19:11-20

Church Age

7yr. Trib

Millennial Kingdom 1,000 yrs. of peace

1. The coming peace treaty between Arabs and Israel
2. Israel's time of peace and prosperity
3. Russia invades Israel and is destroyed by God 3 1/2 years or more before the tribulation

Antichrist signs covenant with Israel for 7 years to start the Tribulation period
Dan. 9:27

Antichrist breaks the covenant in the middle of the Tribulation and persecutes Israel
Rev. 13; II Thess. 2; Dan. 7:25; 9:27b

Whether the rapture of the church takes place *before* the peace treaty is signed, only God knows. It probably will not, so that the church can serve as soul harvesters after God reveals His presence by destroying Russia.

Rapture could take place several years prior to the tribulation period. The closer we get to the actual occurrence of these events, however, the more we are inclined to believe that they could happen in close succession. If they do indeed occur in close proximity or simultaneously, the church will still be on earth when Russia invades Israel and is destroyed by God.

Any chronology of the Rapture and the invasion of Israel is speculative and should be given wide flexibility. However, it is instructive to examine some of the possibilities. One possibility is offered in the third chart.

When Will God Destroy Russia?

Having considered the possibilities for the seven years when the implements of war are burned, we can speculate on the possible time of the invasion of Israel and the subsequent destruction of Russia. Although we know they will take place a minimum of 3 1/2 years before the Tribulation, no one can predict when the Tribulation will occur; the exact time of our Lord's return is known only to God.

I believe that the next major event on the prophetic calendar will be the peace treaty between Israel and the Arab world. This cessation of hostilities may likewise signal a short time of peace throughout the whole world. For example, in speaking of the end time and the coming of Christ, 1 Thessalonians 5:2–3 says that the day of the Lord will come "while people are saying, 'Peace and safety.'" Further, "Destruction will come on them suddenly, as labor pains on a pregnant woman, and they will not escape." This indeed suggests that before the holocaust known as the tribulation period, a time of peace and safety will encompass this earth, interrupted only by Russia's invasion of Israel.

As we noted in an earlier chapter, the generation that saw Israel become a nation will not pass away until the Lord has come, according to Matthew 24. So signs of peace and safety in Israel should appear soon in order that the false period of prosperity which precedes Russia's invasion can begin to take shape. It is impossible to say that such an eventuality will come in the eighties or nineties or even before the dawn of the next

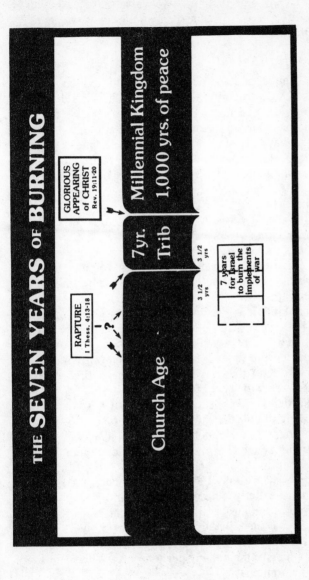

The whole seven years of burning could come *before* the Tribulation begins. It cannot be in the Millennium, for the earth is renovated by fire (2 Peter 3:10—13). The Jews are persecuted during the last 3 1/2 years of the Tribulation, so at least the first 3 1/2 years of that burning will be in the church age. Before or after the Rapture? No one knows.

century. What can be predicted, however, is that Russia will be destroyed before the Antichrist arrives on the scene and signs his covenant with Israel.

Which comes first: Russia's destruction or Christ's return?

There is no simple and dogmatic answer to the question of whether Russia's destruction comes before Christ's return. The Bible does not offer conclusive evidence, and my suggested answer should be regarded as somewhat speculative.

The Rapture may occur in any of four possible time sequences: before Russia is destroyed, immediately afterward, long afterward, or simultaneously with the signing of the covenant between the Antichrist and Israel. Note these four possibilities on the fourth chart.

I personally believe Christ's return will occur after Russia is destroyed, as I explain more fully in the next chapter. I am convinced that the destruction of Russia will appear as a supernatural event that will cause all the world to know that God has acted. During the aftermath of this catastrophe, millions of people will seek the Lord. In fact, the greatest soul harvest in the history of mankind may result from that moment of divine retribution. If so, there will be a need for harvesters; since this event takes place before Israel's conversion and the sealing of the 144,000 during the first half of the Tribulation, who will be better equipped to do the harvesting than the church of Jesus Christ and her worldwide host of missionaries?

I risk the criticism of colleagues when I suggest that Christ may rapture His church *after* the destruction of Russia—particularly because there is no conclusive biblical teaching for this view. I may be influenced by my yearning to see the mighty soul harvest, as related in the next chapter. But I caution the reader not to be dogmatic. We know Russia will be destroyed, but we cannot determine exactly when in the scenario it will happen.

I had an opportunity recently to share this concept with a nationally known Bible scholar whom I have known for many years. He listened patiently and evaluated all the suggested scenarios pertaining to the coming peace treaty. When I finished, he offered two comments.

"Now I understand why you call it the coming peace in the Middle East," he began. Then he added, "The only problem

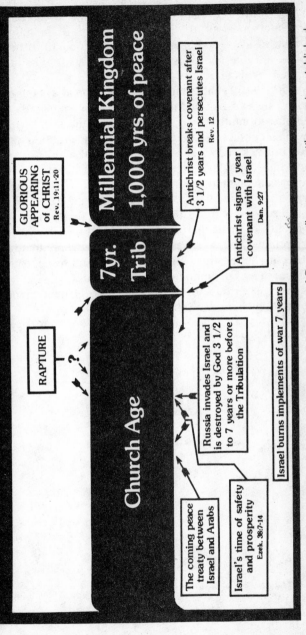

WHEN WILL GOD DESTROY RUSSIA?

Church Age

7 yr. Trib

Millennial Kingdom 1,000 yrs. of peace

RAPTURE

?

GLORIOUS APPEARING of CHRIST
Rev. 19:11-20

Antichrist breaks covenant after 3 1/2 years and persecutes Israel
Rev. 12

Antichrist signs 7 year covenant with Israel
Dan. 9:27

Russia invades Israel and is destroyed by God 3 1/2 to 7 years or more before the Tribulation

Israel burns implements of war 7 years

The coming peace treaty between Israel and Arabs

Israel's time of safety and prosperity
Ezek. 38:7-14

We can only speculate on the date, but the destruction of Russia will not come until peace is established between the Arabs and the Jews, followed by a time of great prosperity in Israel and perhaps the rest of the world—possibly lasting five-to-ten years.

with this entire presentation is that passage in Revelation 20:8 where Satan goes out 'to deceive the nations in the four quarters of the earth—Gog and Magog—to gather them to battle.' If God destroys Russia soon, as you say He will, who are those described in this text?''

I responded, ''That event transpires at least a thousand years later, at the end of the Millennium, when the satanic spirit of rebellion will infiltrate the national world rulers and oppose God in the final conflict. As we have seen, the destruction of Gog and Magog in Ezekiel 38 and 39 is not identical with the destruction of Gog and Magog of Revelation 20, for the events occur at least one thousand and ten years apart.''

Yes, I am inclined to believe that as members of the body of Jesus Christ we will see the destruction of Russia and have an opportunity to share in an unprecedented soul harvest. This is one reason why I challenge Christians everywhere to develop the practice of sharing their faith effectively and to appropriate the maximum means of communication in this day.

As you ponder this possibility, consider the next chapter—the most exciting chapter in this book.

9. The Real Reason Why
God Will Destroy Russia

"I will display my glory among the nations, and all the nations will
see the punishment I inflict and the hand I lay upon them [Gog, the
chief prince of Russia, and the spirit of the evil one that indwells him,
along with Russia and her allies]" (Ezekiel 39:21).

For 1,900 years the God of the universe has been silent—at least
in ways our sophisticated world can understand. The apostle
Peter warned,

First of all, you must understand that in the last days scoffers will
come, scoffing and following their own evil desires. They will say,
"Where is this 'coming' he promised? Ever since our fathers died,
everything goes on as it has since the beginning of creation" (2 Peter
3:3–4).

The secular humanist intellectuals of our day are among the
greatest scoffers the world has ever known. Unless they see a
worldwide flood, a Moses who rolls back the Red Sea, the ten
plagues of Egypt, the daily manna sent down from heaven to
feed three million Jews, the closed mouth of Daniel's lions, or
the fiery furnace that cannot destroy the three Hebrew children,
they will not believe in a supernatural God.

It is easier for these skeptics to look up at the stars and
announce "accident," survey the marvels of nature and proclaim
"spontaneous life," analyze the amazing human body and
conclude "evolution" than to profess "God." The Bible calls
such people fools: "The fool says in his heart, 'There is no God.'
They are corrupt, their deeds are vile; there is no one who does
good" (Psalm 14:1).

153

We have already noted two of God's purposes for destroying the invading armies of Russia and their allies:

1. To judge Magog (Russia) and Gog (the chief prince of Russia and the spirit that drives all evil leaders);

2. To save the nation of Israel politically and spiritually.

Now we should examine the most important reason of all: *"That all the world will know that I am the Lord."* Eight times in Ezekiel 38—39 God announces that this is His true purpose in destroying the invading forces of Russia.

1. "In days to come, O Gog, I will bring you against my land, so that the nations may know me when I show myself holy through you before their eyes. . . .And all the people on the face of the earth will tremble at my presence. The mountains will be overturned, the cliffs will crumble and every wall will fall to the ground" (38:16, 20).

2. "And so I will show my greatness and my holiness, and I will make myself known in the sight of many nations. Then they will know that I am the Lord" (38:23).

3. "I will send fire on Magog and on those who live in safety in the coastlands, and they will know that I am the Lord" (39:6).

4. "I will make known my holy name among my people Israel" (39:7).

5. "I will no longer let my holy name be profaned, and the nations will know that I the Lord am the Holy One in Israel" (39:7b).

6. "I will display my glory among the nations, and all the nations will see the punishment I inflict and the hand I lay upon them" (39:21).

7. "From that day forward the house of Israel will know that I am the Lord their God" (39:22).

8. "When I have brought them back from the nations and have gathered them from the countries of their enemies, I will show myself holy through them in the sight of many nations. Then they will know that I am the Lord their God, for though I sent them into exile among the nations, I will gather them to their own land, not leaving any behind" (39:27–28).

God, in remaining generally silent for the past 1,900 years, has chosen to make the skeptics believe in Him by faith rather than by physical demonstration. The destruction of Russia will be a striking exception.

The Most Memorable Day in Modern History

This world has known many memorable days: the creation of the earth, the flood in the days of Noah, the death and resurrection of Jesus Christ. Since then, nothing in the physical world shows the irrefutable hand of God in terms that the most sophisticated unbeliever can understand.

When our Lord walked on the earth, He performed such mighty miracles that even His greatest enemies had to acknowledge that He was endowed with supernatural power. Thinking people who saw Him walk on water, calm the troubled storms, multiply a boy's lunch to feed thousands of people, heal all manner of diseases, cast out demons, and even raise the dead were forced to admit, "No one could perform the miraculous signs you are doing if God were not with him" (John 3:2).

Infallible miracles vs. ordinary miracles

Luke, the physician who wrote the Book of Acts, called the post-resurrection appearances of Jesus "convincing proofs" ("infallible proofs," KJV) that He was really alive (Acts 1:3). When the apostle Thomas saw the resurrected Christ, he accepted that appearance as undeniable proof (John 20:24–29).

I believe in miracles. In fact, almost all Christians have experienced miracles. I consider it a miracle when 90 percent of the faithful tithing Christian's income goes further than what 100 percent would go if he did not tithe. I have known that miracle in my own life and in those of hundreds of Christians whom I have challenged to be faithful to God economically.

I believe that God can, if He so chooses, heal the sick. One of our own children was given up for dead, but God miraculously spared her life. As a pastor for 30 years, I have encountered many miracles, though I do not understand why God does not choose to heal all individuals who are sick. Many of the people I have prayed for have died, whereas some have lived miraculously. The skeptical mind is seldom convinced by any of these events we call miracles.

For instance, my wife and I will always believe that God performed a miracle when our son, Lee, at age four was run over by a car, yet suffered no broken bones or permanent injury. An unsaved person looks at such an event and announces "coincidence"; it is not understood as an "infallible proof" of the existence of God.

In His sovereignty God has chosen for nearly twenty centuries to require that man believe in Him through the printed or spoken word of God and through the power of the Holy Spirit. During this period of time, He has performed millions of ordinary miracles, but to my knowledge, at no time has He provided an "infallible proof" miracle—one that would force even the greatest skeptic to acknowledge the supernatural existence of God.

However, one day God *will* perform an "infallible proof" miracle—the destruction of Russia's invading armies on the mountains of Israel. No wonder He calls it *"a memorable day"* (Ezekiel 39:13), for on that day He will be glorified in the eyes of "the whole world." The Sovereign Lord will intervene at a climatic time in world history and instantly solve one of its greatest problems by completely eliminating Russian Communism. In one dynamic moment He will judge Russia, save Israel, and prove to the most skeptical minds that a supernatural God exists. I can grieve over the enormous loss of human life that such an event will cause; but I can also rejoice in God's willingness to manifest His supernatural power so that all the world will know that He is the Lord.

That "memorable day" will spark in many a personal belief in the existence of an omnipotent God. The skeptical nations and even the skeptics living in Israel will believe. The result will be the greatest soul harvest in history.

The Coming Soul Harvest

The God I have learned to love through the study of His Word and more than thirty years of service is not primarily a God of judgment. He is a God who loves mankind and whose supreme desire is to bring man into fellowship with Himself. That is why He sent His only begotten Son. That is also why, although He is merciful, He will dramatically interfere in the affairs of men and nations to reveal that He is Lord. Through the medium of television, every country of the world will receive the electrifying news that God has destroyed the invading armies of Russia.

The aftermath of such an event can only fulfill the purpose of God when the millions of souls who have been deceived by secular humanist philosophy suddenly realize that a supernatural God reigns over the universe. I have no question that literally multiplied millions will be driven to their knees to call upon the name of the Lord. Those who have heard the gospel prior to that time may spontaneously look to the Lord for salvation. Others will need the printed page, the Word of God, church services, television and radio programming, and personal witnessing.

Can you imagine the exciting opportunities that await us on your first day back to work after that "memorable day"? Suppose you have been sharing your faith with three or four skeptics—worldly wise sophisticates who deny the eternal existence of God. They will assuredly be filled with questions that no television commentator can answer. If you are the only Christians in whom they have confidence, they will naturally turn to you with their questions. You must be prepared. You may explain that this in not "the day of the Lord"—a moment of judgment—but the age of grace, so they can yet call upon the name of the Lord and be saved. But you can also assure them that time is short, for in all likelihood only a very brief period will separate the destruction of Russia and the rapture of the church.

That is why I urge Christians everywhere to learn how to share their faith in the power of the Holy Spirit. We should practice it vigorously now so that we can be skilled in the use of the Word of God when that memorable day comes. I encourage you to make a prayer list of specific individuals, relatives, friends, neighbors, and associates whom you want to see come to Christ. Start praying for them now, for in all likelihood these events will occur during our lifetime. But don't make the mistake of waiting until that day to share your faith. Some of your loved ones may not live till then. Moreover, you will want to sow the seed so that it can come to harvest immediately after that day.

One reason why I have maintained a heavy load of work under intense pressure in recent years—including laying the foundation for a national television ministry—is because of the coming "memorable day." If it occurs in my lifetime, I want to be working in the greatest medium known to mankind, communicating the gospel of salvation to an empty world. Currently that medium is television. Whether we have one day or two years after that memorable day to proclaim the gospel, I want to spend my energies and creativity doing it. Today we must sow the seed for that eventual opportunity of harvest. Those who have established the largest, most durable platform will reach the greatest number of people during that short period. We must start building our platforms under God's direction now.

Admittedly, not all the world will be saved as a result of those dramatic events, but many people will be. If these events occur within the next decade and five billion people inhabit this planet earth (as expected), it is conceivable that 20 percent could receive the Lord. That would mean a soul harvest of one billion people in a very short period of time, a figure unknown in history.

Soul harvest, not revival

We must not be confused about these future events. They are not harbingers of a worldwide revival. In fact, nothing in the prophetic Scriptures indicates that the world will get better and better at the end time. Instead, it teaches quite the opposite—that "perilous times will come" (2 Timothy 3:1, KJV)

In the same way that the skeptical Pharisees of Jesus' day observed His supernatural demonstrations of power and rejected Him, so millions of people will spurn the truth after God's striking intervention in that day. We may hope that more than a billion souls will call upon the name of the Lord, but what about the other three-to-four billion people on the earth? Very likely, the majority will heed the lying devices of Satan and begin to explain away those supernatural events—for in the final analysis it is not enough just to believe in the supernatural power of God. One must repent of his sins and surrender his will to God—and that humble gesture clashes with man's innate sense of pride.

No human being can long entertain the conflict of mind between what he truly believes and what he does. For example, many people reject the Lord today, not for lack of evidence, but for love of sin. As Peter has warned, "Scoffers will come, . . .following their own evil desires." And rather than give up self-love to follow their beliefs, many will change their beliefs to justify their lusts.

During the crucial days after this memorable moment in world history, there will be two realms of action: the political and the

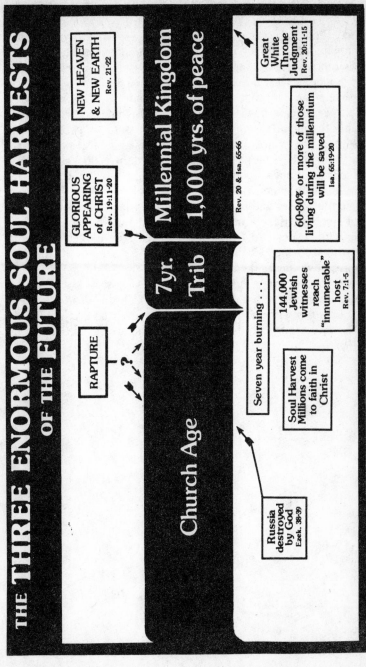

THE THREE ENORMOUS SOUL HARVESTS OF THE FUTURE

RAPTURE

GLORIOUS APPEARING of CHRIST Rev. 19:11-20

NEW HEAVEN & NEW EARTH Rev. 21-22

Church Age

7yr. Trib

Millennial Kingdom 1,000 yrs. of peace

Great White Throne Judgment Rev. 20:11-15

Rev. 20 & Isa. 65-66

Russia destroyed by God Ezek. 38-39

Soul Harvest Millions come to faith in Christ

Seven year burning . . . .

144,000 Jewish witnesses reach "innumerable" host Rev. 7:1-5

60-80% or more of those living during the millennium will be saved Isa. 66:19-20

After God destroys Russia, "all the world" will know that He is "the Lord," and millions will turn to Him. This soul harvest will last from one day to several years, depending on when the Rapture takes place. Further evidence of God's love is that there will be another great soul harvest during the Tribulation.

spiritual. Politically, as we have already seen, the world will amalgamate into a universal kingdom and prepare for the reign of the Antichrist. How long that will take no one knows; it is doubtful whether it will extend to more than a decade.

In that same era, many people will come to grips with the spiritual significance of the events and come to salvation. Probably the majority will not. The current status of people who will witness the events of that day determines in large part what they will do then. If they have already heard the gospel countless times and have not responded to it, they likely will not respond then either. Abraham said to Lazarus in Luke 16:31, "If they do not listen to Moses and the Prophets, they will not be convinced even if someone rises from the dead." Probably the billion or so people who respond to Christ in the great soul harvest will be those who are being deceived now about the existence of God or who have never heard the truth.

If we confess with our mouths that "Jesus is Lord" and believe in our hearts that God raised Him from the dead, we are saved. For it is with the heart that we believe and are justified, and it is with the mouth that we confess and are saved (Romans 10:9–10).

10. Is America in Bible Prophecy?

One question recurs with increasing frequency as Russia becomes a more dominant world power: "Is America mentioned in Bible prophecy?" With so many nations of the end time mentioned by name—Egypt, Persia, Iran, Libya, Israel, Russia, and others—it seems reasonable to most students of prophecy that a nation like the United States must be included. Because of America's unique biblical heritage, God's obvious blessing on this country throughout her three-hundred-year history, her worldwide missionary enterprises, and her stature in the world, why wouldn't God include some mention of America during the last days?

Bizarre Speculations

Through the years I have heard some wild ideas expressed in strange places. Many years ago, as a very young pastor in Minneapolis, I attended a great prophecy conference supported by more than a hundred churches. One speaker devoted an evening to Revelation 17 and 18, focusing on the destruction of Babylon. He concluded that "the city of Babylon is none other than New York City." He went to great lengths describing how the entire city is built on a fault that could crack during an earthquake, causing it to vanish into the sea—and thus fulfill the prophecies about Babylon.

America is not Babylon, and neither is New York City. If I had written my book *Revelation—Illustrated and Made Plain* back then, I would have given him a copy, for in it I confirm that the ancient city of Babylon will be rebuilt and become the capital of the world religiously, politically, and economically. Then, at the end of the Tribulation, God will supernaturally destroy Babylon—"that great city."

I predict that other bizarre theories about America will increase as we approach the twenty-first century. The closing out of two millennia after Christ appears to have great significance, for God's timeclock seems to function in one-day units: to Him a day is merely "a thousand years." Historically there was a renewed interest in Bible prophecy just before the year 1000, and I expect the same to occur in the remaining eighties and the nineties. Before the year 2000, many of the end-time prophecies of Daniel, Matthew, and Revelation may be fulfilled.

The British Israel theory that began to gain a strong following in the nineteenth century is another example of misguided speculation. It encompasses a variety of views, but typically it declares that the sons of Isaac migrated to Great Britain and the United States and the Anglo-Saxon race has become the inheritor of the promises of God to Israel. This belief distorts many prophetic passages of Scripture.

According to the golden rule of biblical interpretation, "When the plain sense of Scripture makes common sense, seek no other sense, but take every word at its primary literal meaning unless the facts of the immediate text studied in the light of related passages and axiomatic and fundamental truths indicate clearly otherwise."[1]

False Thinking About America

The belief that America is not referred to explicitly in the Bible takes some Christians by surprise, for we Americans have a tendency to think of our country as a nation of destiny. The fact is, however, that although we may perceive an allusion or an inference in some prophetic passages, there is no clear-cut reference to America in all the Bible.

On the one hand we reject the British Israelite theory, but on the other we presume that God has blessed this country because

----

[1]David L. Cooper, founder, Biblical Research Society, Los Angeles, California.

it was particularly chosen by Him to be His torchbearer in these last two centuries. It seems incredible that a nation so prominent in the last days would not be mentioned somewhere by the prophets.

> "Sheba and Dedan and the merchants of Tarshish and all her villages will say to you, 'Have you come to plunder? Have you gathered your hordes to loot, to carry off silver and gold, to take away livestock and goods and to seize much plunder?'" (Ezekiel 38:13).

If an allusion to America appears in Bible prophecy, this is it. If Bible scholars are right and "Tarshish," "Sheba," and "Dedan" represent the Phoenician seafarers who migrated to Great Britain before the time of Christ, America is obliquely referred to here. But I am persuaded that if God really intended to include America in biblical prophecy, He would have been more explicit.

I have read various nationalistic and patriotic statements to the effect that God chose America to be settled by God-fearing people of courage so that He could shower blessings on us which were originally intended for the nation of Israel. As much as I love the United States, I find that theory suspect. First, there is no scriptural evidence for such an idea. Second, it tends to make America the recipient of the covenant promises given to Israel, which is unwarranted biblically. Third, if America does not experience a moral revival soon, her exportation of evil will soon exceed her exportation of the good news of the gospel.

I am not unaware of the testimony of Christopher Columbus and his divine vision regarding the discovery of the Americas. I am familiar with the enormous investments many dedicated American patriots have made in this nation and still are making. Many Christians and other Americans are as fully devoted to the preservation of this nation as any of her founding fathers. If the nation does not regain her moral sanity, it will not be the fault of these patriotic citizens. But we have to look somewhere other than biblical prophecy for the role America plays in the world.

What Is the Secret of America's Greatness?

We need to understand why God has blessed America. It isn't because of her humanitarian treatment of the Indians who preceded us, nor is it for her record on slavery. But she has catalogued a very positive record in several other matters that have incurred the favor of God. Actually the United States has done more things right in the building of the nation than wrong, and God has blessed accordingly.

1. Biblical principles and acknowledgment of God

No matter how zealously present-day secular humanist educators try to distort American history, they cannot alter the fact that America was rooted in more biblical principles than any nation in the history of the world. Why? Because it was founded by more dedicated Christians than any other nation. Atheists do not pioneer the building of a new nation in pursuit of freedom, and enduring the hazards of pioneering is not their style. They prefer to let the Christians build a nation. Then they infiltrate her; alter her laws; take over her government, media, and school system; and change her culture to conform to their humanistic ideas. This has been their program in America, and that is why the nation is currently living on the outskirts of Sodom and Gomorrah.

The Declaration of Independence and most of the other founding documents contain clear recognition of God. The nation's laws are filled with biblical values because the framers of the Constitution were themselves either Christians committed to the Word of God or citizens whose thinking process was saturated with basic Christian values. As Dr. Francis Schaeffer says, they had a "Christian conscience." Most of them came from the part of Europe that had been greatly influenced by the Reformation.

I believe our forefathers clearly intended to incorporate Christian or biblical values in all phases of American life. In so doing, they incurred the blessing of God.

God loves all mankind. He will bless any nation that obeys Him; nationality does not influence His administration of grace. The blessing of God is available to all nations only as a result of obedience. "Blessed rather are those who hear the word of God and obey it" (Luke 11:28).

One reason why I have become so vocal in crying out against the changes imposed on our nation during the last twenty-five years is that most of them conflict with the teaching of the Word of God. If this nation does not halt the secularizing trends of the sixties and seventies, she will soon be as godless as Russia, China, India, Babylon, Persia, and Rome.

2. Religious freedom

Historically governments and political leaders have been hostile to religion, particularly religious freedom. Because Americans have enjoyed more religious freedom than any nation in history, we have taken it for granted. In the eighties, however, we have experienced more attacks on religious freedom than any of us thought possible just a few years ago. Who would have believed that the IRS would harass Christian schools? Or that churches could lose their tax deductible status and be forced to pay taxes? Or that government bureaucrats would interfere with the rights of parents to enforce religious values in the raising of their children? Or that a Christian college could be disciplined by the Supreme Court for its interpretation of the Bible regarding interracial marriage? Or ministers could be jailed for running a Christian school in accordance with religious values instead of government values? The list is long.

Our nation's original respect for God, the Bible, and the church incurred the blessing of God for three hundred years of colonial and national history. How else can we explain the victories of the Revolutionary War and the War of 1812? Humanly speaking, our nation snatched victory from the jaws of defeat. We can only account for such events in the light of the blessings of God.

3. Praying, Spirit-filled Christians

Before God decided to destroy Sodom and Gomorrah, He and Abraham engaged in an interesting conversation (Genesis 18:20–33). God agreed to spare the city for forty, twenty, and then ten righteous souls. Unfortunately Sodom and Gomorrah were destroyed because they did not have ten righteous residents. From that account I believe we may draw the premise that God's blessing is extended to a nation in proportion to the percentage of her population that is truly born again. If that be true, America can trace many of her blessings to the fact that she has always had a higher percentage of born-again Christians among her population than any other country.

At this stage in American history, it is difficult to say whether that reality will offset the national holocaust created by liberal abortion laws that account for the death of 1.5 million unborn babies each year.

4. America's benevolence and role as peacemaker

Jesus said in Matthew 5:9, "Blessed are the peacemakers, for they will be called sons of God." In 1945 America's military machine conquered Germany and Japan and could easily have gone on to conquer the world. Instead she helped her former enemies rebuild their shattered nations until they were economically her greatest competitors in the world marketplace. In all of history there has never been a more "merciful" nation. God has blessed the United States, not because she is a nation of destiny, but because she has been compassionate.

To a lesser extent, the United States has also been a peacemaking nation until the last few years. Then liberal humanists in power caused her to retreat from her responsibilities and permit Communism to enslave millions. Her failure to give Gen. Douglas MacArthur permission to defend Korea from invasion by Chinese Communists permitted the enslavement of forty million Koreans. Her failure to use military might in Vietnam was a national disgrace, permitting the enslavement or murder of twenty million people. Her vain attempt to enforce the Monroe Doctrine in 1962 permitted Comrade Castro to terrorize many countries in Latin America and even Angola in southwestern Africa. That failure has led to the suffering, murder, and displacement of at least twenty million people.

Before the adoption of this weak foreign policy, the United States enjoyed the blessing of God as a peacemaking nation. Unfortunately the left-wing and humanistic policymakers in the State Department seem to believe that national weakness for us in the face of Communist Russia's inhuman program of world conquest is a virtue. But that flies in the face of both history and common sense. In Luke 11:21–22 Jesus taught the opposite.

"When a strong man, fully armed, guards his own house, his possessions are safe. But when someone stronger attacks and overpowers him, he takes away the armor in which the man trusted and divides up the spoils."

This sounds like the familiar motto "peace through strength."

5. Her national policy toward Israel

Of all the reasons why God has blessed America, none is more significant than her three-hundred-year history of benevolence toward the Jews. God promised Abraham, "I will bless those who bless you, and whoever curses you I will curse; and all peoples on earth will be blessed through you" (Genesis 12:3). No other nation in history has exceeded her record of charity extended to the sons of Abraham, Isaac, and Jacob. I consider this America's best line of national defense.

Let me explain this. Some people complain that Israel receives too much from the United States' defense budget—more than $4 billion in 1983. These people suggest that we would better serve our nation by giving that money to the poor or to a larger nation. But I believe that the stronger we make Israel, the safer we are as a nation.

One reason is that no one knows how powerful the Soviet Union really is. Even our intelligence-gathering services—hampered as they are by congressional restraints — are unreliable, as the Grenadan invasion of 1983 disclosed. It would be possible for a U.S. president to be blackmailed into submitting to a Communist takeover out of fear of Russian supremacy. The Communists are consummate bluffers and masters of "misinformation." The tragedy of the twentieth century could well be the unnecessary capitulation to Communist slavery by naive leaders in the United States in the face of what they thought was nuclear superiority and first-strike destruction, but in reality was a paper tiger.

As long as there is a strong Israeli air force with the capability of nuclear retaliation, Russia will not attack the United States. Israel is the Achilles' heel to the Soviets' designs for world supremacy. Before they can suppress the world with their totalitarian ideology, they must first knock out the United States. And to do that, they must first remove Israel.

Thus Israel's safety and military strength are our own nation's best interest for survival. Why should we not supply them with F-15s and F-16s, our latest weapons systems, air-to-air refueling capabilities, and even missiles, ICBMs, or anything else that makes Israel a threat to Russia? It is not that Russia (the No. 1

superpower) has need to fear Israel (the third most powerful military force) herself; rather, she must fear Nos. 2 and 3 simultaneously.

Another reason is that, although we spend less in the defense of Israel than we do in Europe and Japan, we get a greater return on our investment. Europe has as many people as the United States, but she seems to have little stamina for standing up to the Soviet Union. Her leaders criticize us when we oppose the Communists. When U.S. marines invaded Grenada, for example, we received nothing but abuse from our European allies.

And what about our Japanese allies, whom the United States has been protecting from Chinese and Russia communism for four decades? Because of American aid, Japan has been able to divert its resources and technology from the national defense to consumer goods—automobiles, radios, and computers—often to the detriment of our own economy.

Of all our allies, Israel is the only one we can depend on in a time of crisis. Why? (1) Because our survival is vital to her own; (2) because there are three times as many Jews in the United States as there are in Israel; and (3) because she is the only other nation besides ours that has the potential for military retaliation against a Russian attack.

We get more results from the dollars we spend in building a strong defense for Israel than we do from any others. Israel has already demonstrated its will to fight when attacked. We don't have to agree with everything Israel does to realize that defending her is a good investment in our own best interests.

I further believe that we as a people have enjoyed more years of free elections—more than two hundred years of them—than any other nation. We have experienced more religious freedom and more prosperity, because we have recognized that the Jews are God's chosen people and the special objects of His love—not because they deserve it, but because He chose them even before the first Jew, Jacob, was born. Jews were welcomed in America during her colonial days and have enjoyed more freedom here than they have ever been granted before. That no doubt explains why at least 55 percent of the world's Jews reside in America. There are almost as many Jews in New York City (3 million) as in Israel (3.5 million).

In the United States, Jews share the rights and privileges of all her citizens. They can freely own land, run for public office, enjoy unparalleled religious freedom, manage banks and businesses, and live a discrimination-free life. The little persecution of Jews that occurs is always met with community outrage, and the courts and law enforcement officers restrain such individuals. Anti-Semitism is not condoned in this country, and one hopes it never will be.

Christians—Israel's Best Friend

It is no accident that the country with the world's best treatment of the Jews was founded on more Christian principles than any other nation and has more Christians (69 million: Gallup Poll) than any other. Born-again Christians who know their Bible have always been Israel's best friend. Admittedly, some in history who were identified as Christians have persecuted the Jews, but they were not biblically taught. True believers recognize God's covenant with Israel and use their influence to perpetuate the national humanitarian treatment of them as a people, thus incurring the blessing of God.

America to the rescue, 1940–1945

I was never more proud of my country than when I stood at the museum in a German concentration camp in Dachau, Germany, studying the photographs of the atrocities inflicted there under the Nazi regime. Adolf Hitler began imprisoning the Jews in 1936. Pictures taken on the way to captivity show them plump, well-dressed, and not seriously concerned. The pictures of 1938 testify that the imprisonments intensified and the starvation and persecution of the inmates increased. By 1945 the Jews were literally skeletons with skin but without flesh. However, the haunting looks on those emaciated faces suddenly turned to excited joy. What had happened? American GIs had come to rescue them.

The United States has not only provided a welcome haven for Jews in our homeland, but has rescued three-fourths of the world's Jews from certain annihilation. That mad dictator, Hitler, intended to wipe out all the Jews in Europe and Russia. At that time, three-fourths of the world's Jews lived within the borders of the countries Hitler would have conquered—if America had not entered the war.

There is no question in my mind that we have enjoyed unprecedented blessing from God in this country because of our treatment of the Jews. How long that character will offset the humanist-inspired practices of abortion on demand, homosexual acceptance, pornography, and continual secularization of our society I do not know. But in my heart I am convinced that if we ever change our policy toward the Jews, we will become like Sodom and Gomorrah.

Israel right or wrong?

The national policy of the United States toward Israel does not support everything that nations does. We Christians must remember that many of Israel's leaders are Zionists; consequently some of them are as secular as America's humanists. If some Zionists had their way, they would close the synagogues and do away with many time-honored Jewish customs. In addition, Zionist-inspired dealings with the Arab residents of Israel do not always show respect for human rights. If they were to become inhumane in their treatment of the Arabs, the United States would have to reevaluate her policies toward Israel. I hope that we as a people will never be found guilty of mistreating the Jews as individuals.

As a nation, Israel inhabits the land largely in unbelief. Not until Russia is supernaturally destroyed by God on the mountains of Israel will the nation turn en masse to Him. Until then, we must treat Israel as a trusted ally and judge her on the merits of her conduct—but always treating individual Jews with compassion.

What All This Means

We learn from all these experiences that America has historically enjoyed the blessings of God, not because she was a nation of destiny or is mentioned in biblical prophecy, but because our founding fathers were so biblically oriented in their thinking that they established a country whose conduct pleased God. Any other country following these policies will enjoy the same blessings. A good example is Canada. She is second only to the United States in her record of following biblical principles and of favorable treatment of Jews; thus she too has enjoyed the blessings of God.

England, on the other hand, has fallen on hard times after centuries of national blessing. Many prophecy students feel that England turned her back on Israel during the thirties and particularly in 1945 and 1946, when she withdrew entirely from Palestine. Consequently she is reaping the results today. In addition, consider England's record on religious freedom and commitment. Four percent of the English people go to church. The government will not permit the construction of a Christian radio or television station there (whereas the United States has more than one thousand Christian radio stations and more than fifty Christian TV stations). Secular humanists exercise more control over national affairs in England than they do in America. That's why their government policy is more secular.

Three confederations of nations

Scripture identifies three confederations of nations in the last days. The two that we have already examined will be involved in the invasion of Israel: the northeastern confederation, consisting of "Russia and her hordes," and the western democracies that send the diplomatic note of Ezekiel 38:13. In all probability Israel is part of the latter confederation, forsaken by her allies just before God intervenes.

Possibly, however, a third confederation may exist at the time of the invasion—or at least a group that will have the capability of being a confederation. "The kings of the East," the nations east of the Euphrates, will march on Israel at the close of the tribulation period, when all the world will attack Christ in "the battle of the great day of God Almighty," known more popularly as the Battle of Armageddon (Revelation 16:12–14). These nations will include China, India, Japan, and other oriental countries. What do they have in common? Eastern religious philosophy—which expresses itself in society in ways similar to secular humanism—and hatred for Christianity and the Bible.

Because the Bible includes these three confederations as players on the world stage in the last days, we can assume that America is included. At present the worldwide presence of the

United States assures that Russia will not rule the world at the end time prior to her attempt to take Israel. The only human instrument that currently keeps Russia from conquering the world is the strength of the United States. This would indicate that America will coexist with Russia right up to the end, but will probably not have any more supremacy over her than we do today. That is, America would be one of the western democracies that sends the diplomatic note to Russia just before the attempted invasion of Israel;

The Future of America

It is not difficult to predict the future of America. Unless we experience a moral revival and shake off the domination of the secular humanists who control our government, media, and public education, we will be a fifth-rate power in twenty-to-thirty years. Does that sound like an extreme statement? I suggest you draw a simple graph of our national decline during the past thirty years and project the same rate of decline for the next thirty. We can apply that graph to the nation's morals, military might, economy, religious freedom, and family breakdown. On the increase are the size of government, taxation, secular humanist propaganda, crime, drugs, VD, pornography, Communist subversion, and a host of other harmful social influences. America will no longer be the America most of us inherited thirty years ago if we continue to decline at the present rate.

The nation's diplomats have negotiated away one-third of the world to Russian communism during the past thirty years. Will another third be enslaved by the year 2000 or 2010? Our taxes have risen from 22 percent of our income after World War II, to 44 percent in 1983. Will it be 88 percent by 2010? or just 66 percent? Inflation has risen more than 300 percent.

Pornography was a $6 billion business in 1983. Herpes and AIDS, two venereal diseases unheard of fifteen years ago, have infected 20.5 million carriers—almost 10 percent of the population. SAT (College Board) scores have plummeted during the period in which the United States increased federal spending for education from $35 billion to $215 billion annually. Crime has risen in these same years by more than 200 percent. America's once invincible military machine has been reduced to a par with Russia's (or maybe even below hers), and the nation's will to defend the country has been decimated. What will it be by the year 2000? The travesty of all travesties is that 16 million unborn babies have been murdered since abortion became legal in all fifty states in 1973. Will the figure rise to 50 million by the year 2000?

The secular humanist policies of the past thirty years will continue as we near the twenty-first century. That America's leaders intend to maintain those policies is spelled out clearly in my books *The Battle for the Mind* and *The Battle for the Family*, in which I quote from the leading secular humanists of our day. They make no attempt to hide their intentions to secularize America totally in the next fifteen years.

Is There Hope for America?

Yes, there is hope for America. As long as life persists, under God we can hope. But that hope will never come to fruition if we continue to violate the moral laws of God.

The only hope for America is a moral revival—a national recognition of her sins against God and her fellowmen and a return to the traditional moral values upon which the nation was founded. I believe that such a revival could happen very soon. Several of the nation's religious leaders have personally expressed to me, in public or in private, a belief that revival is coming.

Something unusual has occurred during the past thirty years in the United States. While she has experienced the moral decline already described, she has also reaped the largest soul harvest and church growth in her history. Surveys suggest that there are almost three times as many born-again Christians in the nation today as there were thirty years ago. The conditions producing this amazing growth may generate three times the soul harvest during the next three decades. If the Gallup Poll is right and the nation indeed has 69 million born-again citizens, that number could jump to 130 million by the year 2000. If that happens, the majority of our population may be Christian by then.

Admittedly, numbers are speculative. But if enough of the

morally committed citizens of the United States will involve themselves in the electoral process by either running for public offices or helping those who share our traditional values get elected, we can rid our government of the secular humanists who are destroying the nation. Such a change in government leadership is possible in one decade, and that is essential to revival, for the humanists in the political and judicial systems have consistently legislated for sin and against civil morality. Currently they seek to stifle religious freedom. The renowned constitutional attorney, William Ball, has stated, "We no longer have religious freedom in this country; we have religious toleration." If Christians do not take a more active part in the electoral process, both as candidates and as campaign workers, these humanists will transform religious toleration into religious intolerance.

Unless we can motivate millions of Christians to realize that politics *is* their business and become as vigorous in getting people of like mind into public office as the secular humanists, we will lose the means of bringing in the revival the nation desperately needs. What are these means?

1. Bible-teaching churches;
2. The electric church—radio and television;
3. Bible translations that people in general can understand;
4. Christian colleges, Bible schools, and seminaries—and a new emphasis on training lawyers, journalists, communications specialists, and educators;
5. Christian publishers producing millions of books and magazines;
6. Christian schools, K–12, that challenge young people to be ministers and missionaries as well as magistrates, journalists, communicators, and educators;
7. Parachurch ministries.

If the humanists seek to keep their control over our society, they will have to destroy these vehicles to the mind or at least limit their freedom. For if the church of Jesus Christ ever awakens to the fact that she constitutes the largest single bloc in America, and if she ever becomes serious about preserving the traditional moral values of the country, she can with God's help break the humanist stranglehold on the nation's media, government, and educational system. This would result in a powerful return to civil moral sanity.

Between now and the twenty-first century, we will see a continuing struggle between secular humanists and Christians. Who knows which side will win? The place to begin is the ballot box. Are you registered to vote? Do you vote? Do you campaign for morally committed candidates? Are you willing to run for office if God so leads? Someone has sagely observed, "He that will not use his freedom to preserve his freedom does not deserve his freedom."

Will Russia Destroy America?

I am frequently asked, "Will Russia conquer the United States before she attempts to invade Israel?" The Bible does not provide an answer, but I have an opinion: "I seriously doubt it." I have stated my reasons already in this book. In short, if America were conquered, nothing could stop Russia from subjugating the whole world. But the prophets make it clear that Russia will attack Israel before a one-world government is formed. I believe that Russia and America will continue to function at parity until Russia becomes powerful enough to defy the U.S. and attack Israel. This will create a vacuum into which the secular humanist advocates of the new world order will move quickly, forming the one-world government of the end time.

Our national policy of humane treatment of the Jews, if unchanged, will keep America from being conquered by Russia. Historically speaking, a nation that was evil to the Jews has never conquered a nation that was good to Israel. The United States' best line of national defense remains her favorable treatment of individual Jews and her national defense of her ally Israel.

Will America Be Destroyed by a Nuclear Bomb?

Again, it is impossible to be dogmatic because the Bible is silent on this subject. However, Christ will return to a well-populated world. I am inclined to believe that the present stalemate of nuclear weapons will continue until the Lord comes. And in that case Christ will come soon. It is frighteningly conceivable that some mad terrorist or Idi Amin–type of dictator could gain control of a nuclear bomb and threaten to destroy the world. The only sure preventative is the second coming of Christ.

The most important words to contemplate on this subject come from our Lord Himself:

> "Therefore keep watch, because you do not know on what day your Lord will come. But understand this: If the owner of the house had known at what time of night the thief was coming, he would have kept watch and would not have let his house be broken into" (Matthew 24:42–43).

11. Did Israel Thwart a Russian Invasion?

All the world was shocked and the United States expressed anger when the Israelis launched a surprise attack on the Palestine Liberation Organization on June 6, 1982. Lebanon, a country with a government too weak to defend itself from invasion and subversion, had served as the unwilling base of terrorist attacks on Israel. Israel had tried to be patient in the face of unprovoked attacks by the PLO that often took the lives of children, but finally they could take it no longer.

By the time the blitzkrieg brought the Israeli army to the outskirts of Beirut, the capital of Lebanon, opinion in the West had turned as the press and major magazines highlighted the extent of the PLO atrocities. Gradually people began to realize that the PLO was in reality a terrorist tool in the hands of the Soviet Union to foment civil strife. The Russians have spawned similar programs in Africa, Cuba, and Central America.

The world was not prepared for the discovery by the Israelis that Russia had secretly stockpiled close to $2 billion worth of military arms and equipment in specially built caverns in the village of Saida near the ruins of the ancient coastal city of Sidon. And all this was in addition to the arms the Russians supplied to the PLO and the Syrians.

Official Israeli government reports gradually coming to light have clearly indicated that the Soviet plans included more than arming the PLO. The Israeli attack caught the Russians by surprise, and a complete inventory of captured weapons revealed that the PLO had far more weapons than troops to man them.

The question arises, Was Russia planning to use this weaponry for the invasion of Israel prophesied in Ezekiel 38–39?

Even the Mossad, the Israeli intelligence agency, was surprised at the extent of the Russian arms buildup in Lebanon. For some time the Mossad had been aware of secret activity in the region, and possibly their intelligence gathering was responsible for the launching of the Israeli attack on the PLO.

Hillare du Berrier, a freelance reporter, wrote in the *Review of the News,*

> Around the village of Saida the largest military base was tunneled out. Steel reinforced caverns and miles of underground galleries were cut through earth and rock to link huge command and storage halls, some of them large enough to shelter fleets of helicopters. . . .
>
> One chamber comprised a vast intelligence storehouse loaded to the ceiling with methodically arranged files. Dossiers on thousands of individuals lined one wall. Rows of shelves held military plans for every conceivable operation and region. A map section covered land areas, ports, and sea bottoms of the world. Significantly, all of the captured documents were in Russian. . . .
>
> The names and records of all Soviet advisors in Lebanon were found in files dating back to the beginning of Soviet/PLO cooperation. Already Mossad has the names of more than 2,000 Europeans and Americans in the Palestinian "foreign legion" along with a library of documentation on terrorists working on the European and American continents under directions from Moscow. More alarming, enough missiles, cannons, tanks, and other armored vehicles to equip a modern army were turned up in the underground depot. A special radar and electronic communications system occupied a self-contained wing of the complex.
>
> Another unexpected discovery in the Soviet fortress beneath Saida was files listing important western firms and personalities who for one reason or another—including blackmail—have been supporting the Palestinian cause politically and financially. [1]

Du Berrier suggests that Israel's assault on Lebanon thwarted a Soviet attack that would have been launched in August—just two months later.

Dr. David Lewis, editor of *Jerusalem Courier* and *Prophecy Digest,* is very knowledgeable about happenings in Israel. As president of the National Christian Leadership Conference for Israel, he has access to the highest leaders in the Israeli

---

[1] "Review of the News" (July 28, 1982).

government. In his book *Magog 1982 Canceled* he recounted his interview with Asher Naim, the Director of the Information Division of the Israeli Government Foreign Ministry.

> Lewis: "We have been reading reports of a huge underground base that has been discovered in Saida [Sidon]. Is that correct?"
>
> Asher Naim: "That is true."
>
> Lewis: "I have some of that report here: 'Lebanon was made the pivot for Moscow's plans for the conquest of the *entire Middle East.* Around the village of Saida the largest *secret military base* in the world was tunneled out. . .steel reinforced caverns. . .*miles* of underground galleries. . .fleets of helicopters. . .ultrasecret chambers. . .steel doors that could only be opened by emissions by radio waves from submarines.' *Is this accurate?*"
>
> Asher Naim: ". . .We pride ourselves on our good intelligence. . . . Even our intelligence was surprised about the magnitude of it." [2]

Dr. Lewis obtained additional details from Gidear Patt, Israeli Minister of Industry and Commerce, during a London press interview.

> We discovered a Russian-made machine which can drill a tunnel of 15 meters in diameter through solid rock in the mountains within a very short time. . . .
>
> After hundreds of meters of one such tunnel we found arms from all over the Soviet bloc. There were some from Saudi Arabia, but the vast majority came from Eastern Europe, including Yugoslavia.
>
> Not only were there weapons in these tunnels for an army of 150,000 (whereas the PLO had only some 15,000 men)—but tents and blankets and food. [3]

I have read several accounts of the capture of a large cache of arms, including tanks and rockets, and a gigantic tunnel digging machine that could easily account for the underground caverns and tunnels that were built from late 1979 until they were discovered in 1982.

One official of the Mossad, who requested not to be identified said, "We knew they were stockpiling arms in the Sidon area,

[2]David Allen Lewis, *Magog 1982 Canceled* (Harrison, Ark.: New Leaf Press, 1982), 14–15.

[3]Ibid., 27.

but we discovered more than 1,000,000 more that we expected.'' Some estimates of eyewitnesses to the network of caverns and tunnels have gone as high as ''military equipment for an army of between 500,000 and a million men.'' Even an army of only 250,000 could be overpowering to a little nation of 3.5 million people.

For reasons known only to military officials high in the Israeli and American governments, a veil of secrecy was placed on information relating to the arms discovery. Although American newspapers referred to an enormous cache of arms captured by the Israelis, no substantial details were given. I read, however, that hundreds of Israeli trucks were needed over several weeks to transport all the equipment to Israel. Another unofficial report indicated that the Jews sold much of the equipment to help finance their operations in Lebanon.

The enormity of this evidence raises many questions. Why would 15,000 PLO terrorists need enough weapons to outfit an army of between 250,000 and 500,000 men? Or why would the PLO require many times more tanks than they had trained tank drivers? Why would they need far more mobile mortars than they had mortar gunners? Why would they need SAM missiles when they had no one capable of firing them?

Only one logical explanation seems to fit: they were stockpiling for an invading army of gigantic size.

The 1982 Russian Strategy

Only three possibilities come to mind as to why the Russians had stockpiled that enormous cache of weapons. It is obvious that they planned some kind of major offensive, and anyone who knows the Communist mind suspects a nefarious plot. Consider these possibilities:

1. A Russian attack on Saudi Arabia

Russia needs oil. The Soviets are self-sufficient at present only because their country is so underdeveloped that they do not use as much as the civilized world. As their country continues to industrialize and modernize, their need for oil will become acute.

Buying foreign oil is not the Soviet style. Saudi Arabia's rather shaky government, internal discord, and impotent army make her situation very unstable, yet she sits on two-thirds of the world's known oil reserves. Quite possibly Russia wanted to use southern Lebanon as a staging area for an airborne invasion of Saudi Arabia. By flying or shipping an army of Russian paratroopers by night, gaining control of strategic oil wells and refineries, a massive ground attack could then be launched from Lebanon, permitting Russia to conquer Saudi Arabia without destroying her oil-producing capabilities.

Can you imagine what control over America and the rest of the Western world this would put into Soviet hands? It is frightening to conceive. Already having sufficient arms on hand for just such an assault, how would the Russians get their troops into Lebanon secretly? By sea? After its invasion of Lebanon, the Israeli army discovered that the Soviets had built a gigantic underground command center supported by reinforced concrete. It comprised a network of tunnels between large storehouses or caverns that accommodated "acres of Russian-built tanks" and thousands of pieces of other heavy military equipment, including large mobile mortars. A series of steel doors controlled by Communist-built computers and installed by German technicians had been under construction since late 1979. It has been estimated that the Israelis captured enough supplies and equipment to supply an army of a half-million. One report indicated that the gigantic steel door to the secret cavern could be activated electrically by a submarine.

In one underground bunker alone, Israeli soldiers captured 70,000 Russian Kalashnikov assault weapons. Yet the PLO army numbered only 6,000 troops.

A reasonable scenario for all this would begin with a secret landing of Soviet tank drivers, mortar and missile troops, and infantry into the caves of Lebanon, followed by a massive airborne invasion of Saudi Arabia with a view to capturing the major oil fields. Then the Soviets would come out of hiding and launch a massive attack from Lebanon on Saudi Arabia while the paratroopers held the strategic positions. In one week or less the Soviets could control two-thirds of the world's oil literally without spilling a drop.

2. *A Russian attempt to take over the Middle East*

The Communists have made no attempt to hide their objective of world conquest. Dr. Fred Schwartz pointed out thirty years ago that the Russian meaning of "peace" was "a piece of this country and a piece of that country." For years the Soviets have tried diligently to seize the key oil-producing countries of the Middle East. It is predictable that Russia may soon tire of trying to dominate the Middle East with unstable Arab surrogates. As I have already pointed out, it is just a matter of time before they decide to do the job themselves.

The scenario I paint for Saudi Arabia could also apply to every other country in the Middle East or North Africa. Russia could easily make an alliance with Syria and commandeer Jordan, Lebanon, Saudi Arabia, Yemen, South Yemen, and Oman in the same way. She could ignore Israel, stabilize her gains, disregard the world's feeble outcries as she did in Afghanistan, and then move into Ethiopia, Somalia, Libya, and Egypt anytime she pleased. Who would stop her? Not the U.S. paper tiger. The liberal humanists in our education system, media, and government have too seriously weakened our will to fight.

Unless the Soviets attack Israel, it is doubtful that the indecisive U.S. state department will resolve to do any more than send a diplomatic note—which Ezekiel predicted we will do when Russia begins her final military invasion. Unless America undergoes a drastic change, we have fought our last war. It is only a matter of time before the philosophy "I'd rather be Red than dead" totally paralyzes our national resolve. In the face of a Soviet takeover of the Middle East, there is little chance of American intervention. But one other possibility remains.

3. *The Russian invasion of Israel*

The secret documents found by the Israelis in the underground command center of Saida clearly show that the Soviets were preparing to launch some kind of massive attack in August 1982. The Jews averted that attack by two months.

Could it have been planned for Israel? Conceivably. In fact, the Russians know that Israel would not sit idly by and permit them to come within forty miles of her borders in order to launch an attack on her Arab neighbors. The Jews would not hesitate to send their F15s and F16s to destroy the entire base. The Soviets know full well that they will have to conquer Israel before they can take over the Middle East by force, so plans for an invasion of Israel for August 1982 are quite credible.

Evidently it was not God's time. The eschatological conditions were not yet right. So the discovery of their plans by Israel has set the Soviets back—temporarily. Perhaps these events will cause the Russians to postpone their plans and resort to diplomacy instead. In fact, the coming peace treaty between the Arabs and the Jews, mentioned in chapter 6, may be the next prophetic event in the Middle East. If so, it will buy the world perhaps five, ten, or fifteen years. But one day soon, when the conditions are just right, God will cause Russia to fulfill the prophecies of Ezekiel 38 and 39—possibly in much the way they seemed to be getting ready in 1982.

We learn a major lesson from the capture of the Russian arms and documents: It is later than we think.

12. How to Prepare for the Future

Written on every heart is the intuitive realization that somehow there is life after death. We don't talk about it much, but everyone thinks about it sooner of later. Sometimes circumstances occur to bring it front and center in our minds.

A thirty-five-year-old man of the world was with his friends at the Colorado River. One member of the party tried to water-ski close to the campsite in an attempt to spray water on the group. Instead he hit a parked boat while he was going about fifty miles an hour; he shot through the air and slammed his head on an overhanging tree. He was killed instantly.

My friend—who rarely contemplated eternity, judgment, sin, or salvation—stayed with the body while the others rushed downriver for help. As he sat by the fire alone, he looked at the lifeless body of his friend covered with a blanket. Needless to say, he was shocked into the reality of thinking about what he rarely considered—life after death.

Jesus Christ had much to say about the future life. He never wasted time debating whether or not humans have an eternal soul that will spend eternity somewhere; He simply assumed it. In fact, He warned several times that man's eternal soul was more important than his physical life. He asked,

> "What good will it be for a man if he gains the whole world, yet forfeits his soul? Or what can a man give in exchange for his soul? For the Son of Man is going to come in his Father's glory with his angels, and then He will reward each person according to what he has done" (Matthew 16:26–27).

Jesus' primary purpose in coming to this earth was to prepare people for eternity, for He said, "I have come that they may have life, and have it to the full" (John 10:10). It was also Christ who told His disciples, "Do not let your hearts be troubled. Trust in God; trust also in me" (John 14:1).

That "heaven," "eternity," "the resurrection," and other terms that bring peace to the heart of man refer to real things can be verified throughout the Bible. Scriptural teachings concerning eternity are credible because they parallel what we all intuitively believe—that there is a different life after physical death.

One day a man came to Jesus and asked, "Good teacher, what must I do to inherit eternal life?" (Mark 10:17). All thinking people have asked that kind of question sometime in life. It is another way of asking, How can I prepare for eternity?

How Can We Prepare for Eternity?

There is only one true way to prepare for our eternal future: "Believe on the Lord Jesus Christ." You may at first be inclined to say, "That is too easy; surely I must do something."

Not really! The difficult part of salvation has all been accomplished. Jesus suffered for our sins, died, and rose again as a testimony that God was satisfied with His sacrifice for sin. Being God in human flesh, He was more than adequate to cleanse the sins of the whole world if they would believe. It wasn't easy, for it cost Him everything. But to us, salvation is free, the gift of God.

If you believe Christ died for your sins and rose again, then acknowledge Him as Lord and Savior of your life. This involves recognizing your status as a sinner and willingness to repent of your self-will and rebellion against God, making Him Lord of your life. You can prepare for your future readily by sincerely praying the following prayer:

> Oh God, I am a sinner, and I believe your Son, Jesus Christ, died for my sins. I need your forgiveness and cleansing; this day I turn my life over to you.

My friend could not erase the water-skiing accident from his mind. When he returned home, he and his wife visited our church in San Diego. Three weeks later he prayed that prayer, committing his life to Jesus Christ. Within a few months his wife prayed similarly. Those prayers not only prepared them for eternity, but laid the foundation for their marriage and their lifestyles, both of which were truly transformed by the experience.

A good friend of mine died recently in an airplane crash. Ten years earlier he had divorced his first wife and five years later married again. After his death it was revealed that he had never changed the beneficiary on his insurance policy. Consequently his present wife and two small children were not covered.

Careless? Yes. Doubtless he had intended many times to modify that policy but just never got around to it. Thankfully, he was better prepared for eternity, for years ago he had invited Christ into his life.

Suppose that had happened to you? Have you prepared for eternity by personally receiving Christ? If you haven't, do it now. And after you have uttered that prayer of repentance, please let me know of your decision.

> Dr. Tim LaHaye
> P.O. Box 16000
> San Diego, CA 92116

How Then Should Christians Live?

Most of the people who read my books have already had the wonderful experience of accepting Jesus Christ as Lord and Savior. What do these rapidly approaching events mean to them?

When I warn Christians that there may be no Western society as we have known it by the year 2000, I certainly do not intend to demotivate them and foster spiritual inactivity. My purpose is to call attention to the fact that the fulfillment of all end-time prophecies is biblically possible in our lifetime.

Consider this: The coming peace treaty between Israel, Russia, and the Arab world which I predict in this book could miraculously occur at any time. Within five years Russia could get greedy and launch her invasion of the tiny Jewish nation and in a single day be destroyed—testifying to all the world that God is alive and well in His heaven and on His earth.

As we have seen, the aftermath of these events would produce the world's greatest soul harvest. The Jews could burn the implements of war for 3 1/2 years, then the Antichrist could set up his world kingdom followed by 3 1/2 years of peace with Israel. The Great Tribulation, which our Lord mentioned in Matthew 24, will occur during the last 3 1/2 years of this age, culminating in the glorious appearing of our Lord and the establishment of His worldwide kingdom for a thousand years. All these events *could* be compressed into just 18 to 20 years.

And what about the Rapture? I *think* it will occur after the destruction of Russia, so that Christians will be on the scene to be the soul-winning harvesters when as much as 20–25 percent of the world's population receives Christ. He *could* come to take away His church *before* that invasion. The Rapture could take place at anytime. Even today.

In a day when materialism, full-color worldliness, humanistic attacks on traditional values, and infidelity abound all around us, we need to live every day in the light of Jesus' imminent coming. Why? Because our purpose in life is to serve God.

The apostle Peter asked a thought-provoking question in the light of the ultimate coming of Christ and the destruction of this present world order.

> Since everything will be destroyed in this way, what kind of people ought you to be? You ought to live holy and godly lives as you look forward to the day of God and speed its coming. . . .So then, dear friends, since you are looking forward to this, make every effort to be found spotless, blameless and at peace with him. (2 Peter 3:11–12, 14).

Our Lord Jesus gave a commandment to us all:

> "Therefore keep watch, because you do not know on what day your Lord will come. But understand this: If the owner of the house had known at what time of night the thief was coming, he would have kept watch and would not have let his house be broken into. So you also must be ready, because the Son of Man will come at an hour when you do not expect him. Who then is the faithful and wise servant? . . . (Matthew 24:42–45).

The answer to the question Jesus asks is the one who is ready. The one who lives a holy life, filled with His Spirit and available to serve Him at any time. If Jesus came *today,* would you be ready to meet Him? We should all live every day as if this were the day of His coming. That way we will not be ashamed or embarrassed by what He finds us doing.

Dr. M. R. DeHaan, renowned Bible teacher of a past generation, had a two-word motto on the wall of his study. It read simply "Perhaps Today." It is my prayer that you will make that your daily motto until He comes—which could well be in our lifetime.